Watch and Pray

How to Pray Effectively During the Eight Prayer Watches

United in Christ Ministries
of Canton

All Scripture quotations, unless otherwise indicated, are taken from the New King James Version. Copyright © 1982 by Thomas Nelson Inc. Used by permission. All rights reserved.

Scripture quotations marked NIV are from the Holy Bible, New International Version®. NIV® Copyright © 1973, 1978, 1984 by International Bible Society. Used by permission of Zondervan. All rights reserved.

"Scripture quotations are from The ESV® Bible (The Holy Bible, English Standard Version®), copyright © 2001 by Crossway, a publishing ministry of Good News Publishers. Used by permission. All rights reserved."

Scripture quotations marked (NLT) are taken from the Holy Bible, New Living Translation, copyright © 1996. Used by permission of Tyndale House Publishers, Inc., Wheaton, IL 60189 USA. All rights reserved.

Scripture quotations marked KJV are taken from The Holy Bible: King James Version, Thomas Nelson, Inc., 1988.

Watch and Pray: Understanding How to Pray Effectively During the Eight Prayer Watches

ISBN-13: 978-1718805170
ISBN-10: 1718805179

Copyright © 2018 United in Christ Ministries of Canton
https://unitedinchristcanton.org

Contents

INTRODUCTION 5
INTERCESSORY PRAYER 17
   CHAPTER ONE 19
PRAYER FOR HEALING 29
   CHAPTER TWO 31
PRAYER OF THANKSGIVING 41
   CHAPTER THREE 43
PRAYER OF PETITION 49
   CHAPTER FOUR 51
PRAYER FOR GOD'S JUSTICE 57
   CHAPTER FIVE 59
PRAYER FOR PROTECTION 65
   CHAPTER SIX 67
SPIRITUAL WARFARE PRAYER 75
   CHAPTER SEVEN 77
PRAYER FOR DIRECTION 83
   CHAPTER EIGHT 85
PRAYER FOR FORGIVENESS 91
   CHAPTER NINE 93
PRAYER FOR SALVATION 101
   CHAPTER TEN 103
PRAYER FOR REPENTANCE 107
   CHAPTER ELEVEN 109
PRAYER FOR BOLDNESS 115
   CHAPTER TWELVE 117
ABOUT THE AUTHOR 123
ENDNOTES 125

Introduction

Prayer is key to our survival as Believers in Jesus Christ. Because of Christ's work on the cross, we have access to God, our Heavenly Father, and the privilege to communicate our needs and desires to Him. We cannot live a healthy spiritual life without prayer, yet, prayer is one aspect of the Christian life that many struggle with for various reasons.

Some Christians become discouraged when their prayers are not immediately answered. They assume that either God is not listening or He does not care. Others may receive an immediate response to prayer, but the answer is not what they expected. And, they miss out on the blessings God has for them because they failed to receive the way He chose to answer their prayer.

In praying that God's will takes precedence in the situations for which we are praying, we are following the example Jesus Christ set for us. On the night of His arrest and betrayal, Jesus went to the Garden of Gethsemane to pray because He knew what He was about to face. In agony, Jesus prayed to His Father to allow "this cup"—or His tragic death—to pass from Him. However, Jesus knew that to save His own life meant that the human race would be eternally separated from God. So, Jesus did not pray to have His way in the matter, but He prayed that God's eternal plan and purpose be done through His death on the cross (Luke 22:42). If Jesus prayed for God's will to be done—in the most extreme circumstances—how much more should we pray that God's plans and purposes be carried out in our lives?

To avoid becoming discouraged or worried that somehow we are not praying correctly or in a way that God will answer, we must learn how to pray effectively so that we can always keep in step with God and what He wants to do in our lives. What does it mean to "pray effectively?" To pray effectively means that we ask the Holy Spirit to help us pray so that God answers our petitions and His plans and purposes are carried out in our lives.

How to Pray

When we are uncertain about what form of prayer to pray, all we have to do is ask: "Lord, show me what to pray and how to pray Your will in this matter," and our Heavenly Father will show us how to pray. In fact, we see examples in the Bible where God tells His people exactly what to pray. In Numbers 6:22-27, for instance, God tells Moses what He wants Israel's priests to pray when they bless the Israelite nation:

> And the Lord spoke to Moses, saying: "Speak to Aaron and his sons, saying, 'This is the

way you shall bless the children of Israel. Say to them: "The Lord bless you and keep you; The Lord make His face shine upon you, and be gracious to you; the Lord lift up His countenance upon you, and give you peace.'" "So they shall put My name on the children of Israel, and I will bless them."

This "Priestly Blessing" is still prayed by both Jews and Christians today. Another well-known prayer that is recited around the world is "the Lord's Prayer," found in Matthew 6:19-13 and in Luke 11:2-4. Knowing that Jesus prayed all of the time, one of Jesus' disciples asked Him to teach them how to pray. Jesus did not hesitate to answer their request then, and He is just as willing today to teach us how to pray in His Name.

When to Pray

The Bible shows us that there are times set aside specifically for prayer. According to Bible commentators, the Israelites prayed three times a day: evening, morning and noon. In Psalm 55:17, David said he prayed three times a day and believed that God heard him. We see where the prophet, Daniel also prayed to God three times a day, even when it placed his life in danger:

> Now when Daniel learned that the decree had been published, he went home to his upstairs room where the windows opened toward Jerusalem. Three times a day he got down on his knees and prayed, giving thanks to his God, just as he had done before (Daniel 6:10, NIV).

The book, *Watch and Pray: Understanding the Eight Prayer Watches*, by United in Christ Ministries of Canton (Michigan), teaches us that whatever time we pray, there is a specific "watch" associated with it. What is a watch? In the Bible, a watch was a period of time in which soldiers were posted at various entry points of their cities to look out for danger or trouble, typically at night. Watches were divided into hours so that cities would have guards posted 24 hours a day.

In a way, this is what we do when we pray. We are watching out for others by praying for them during certain times of the day and night. In fact, this is what we refer to as a "prayer watch." According to *Watch and Pray: Understanding the Eight Prayer Watches*, a prayer watch is a specific time of the day or night to pray the purposes and plans of God. The book further says:

> Prayer watches are normally set in three-hour intervals around the clock beginning at sundown or 6:00 p.m. This results in a total of eight prayer watches. Each prayer watch is a time to pray for yourself, family

members, friends, individuals, businesses, nations, governments, God's righteous judgments, and to prevent Satan from carrying out his diabolical plans. The Holy Spirit will direct our prayers, if we allow Him to, so that we can pray the mind of God and in accordance to His perfect will. Today, God places believers in Jesus Christ in the position of watchmen.[1]

The time periods of the eight prayer watches are listed below:

- **First Prayer Watch:** 6:00 p.m. – 9:00 p.m.
- **Second Prayer Watch:** 9:00 p.m.–12:00 midnight
- **Third Prayer Watch:** 12:00 midnight – 3:00 a.m.
- **Fourth Prayer Watch:** 3:00 a.m. – 6:00 a.m.
- **Fifth Prayer Watch:** 6:00 a.m. – 9:00 a.m.
- **Sixth Prayer Watch:** 9:00 a.m. – 12:00 noon
- **Seventh Prayer Watch:** 12:00 noon – 3:00 p.m.
- **Eighth Prayer Watch:** 3:00 p.m. – 6:00 p.m.

This book is a companion to *Watch and Pray: Understanding the Eight Prayer Watches* by United in Christ Ministries of Canton (Michigan) and focuses on specific times to pray, as well as different types of prayers we can pray during the eight prayer watches. However, this does not mean that we must be rigid in our prayer life and only pray at certain times. There are some prayers, such as intercessory prayers and prayers for healing, that can—and should—be prayed at any time and immediately when someone asks us to pray. However, there are times when we find ourselves praying certain types of prayers at particular times of the day and night, such as petitioning prayers and prayers of protection.

Praying in Faith

For us to be effective in our prayers and receive the answer God wants to give us, we must pray in faith. James 1:6-7 says, "…But let him ask in faith, with no doubting, for he who doubts is like a wave of the sea driven and tossed by the wind. For let not that man suppose that he will receive anything from the Lord."

The Hebrew word for "faith" (emunah) means "firmness," "steadfastness," and "trust." The Bible says in Hebrews 11:6 (NIV), "And without faith it is impossible to please God, because anyone who comes to him must believe that he exists and that he rewards those who earnestly seek him." So, to pray in faith means that we are placing our confidence in God—and not in ourselves—to receive answers to prayer. To please God, we must have a firm, steady trust that He will use His power on our behalf or on behalf of those for whom we are praying. The apostle James says that a prayer of faith, or a prayer offered in faith to God, can restore a sick person: "And the prayer of faith shall save the sick, and the Lord shall raise him up..." (James 5:15a). *Barnes' Notes on the New Testament* explains that the "prayer of faith" is a prayer offered in faith or in the exercise of confidence in God.[2] The commentary goes on to say:

> It is not said that the particular form of the faith exercised shall be that the sick man will certainly recover; but there is to be unwavering confidence in God, a belief that He will do what is best, and a cheerful committing of the cause into His hands. We express our earnest wish, and leave the case with Him.[3]

There will be times, however, when our faith in God may waver because we have not received an answer to our prayers. And, when we do not see any natural evidence of our prayers being answered, it is easy for us to become discouraged and doubt that God will answer our prayers. Instead of walking by faith, as the apostle Paul encourages us to do in 2 Corinthians 5:7, we are focusing on what we can see with our eyes. According to *Barnes' Notes on the New Testament*, God "cannot be pleased with the man who has no confidence in him, who doubts the truth of his declarations and promises."[4]

We should, instead, seek God and ask Him if there is anything in our lives—or the lives of those for whom we are praying— that is preventing our prayers from being answered. We must have faith that God, in His graciousness, will show us what the issue is—if there is one—and be willing to do whatever He reveals to us that would help us pray more effectively.

We honor God when we place our faith and confidence in Him. Hebrews 11:6 clearly says, "But without faith it is impossible to please him: for he that cometh to God must believe that he is, and that he is a rewarder of them that diligently seek him." Sadly, however, we often limit God; and because of our unbelief, God will not work in our situation. Jesus' ministry in Nazareth was hindered because of the unbelief of the people in the city, "Now He did not do many mighty works there because of their unbelief" (Matthew 13:58). We cannot be a benefit to others unless we first gain their trust and confidence. So it is with God. God wants us to trust that He will do what He has said in His Word and in His revealed will to us. So, our faith must not only be rooted in God as we pray, but also in His Word.

Praying God's Word

The Bible is a valuable resource that improves and enhances our prayers and guides the believer in praying according to God's will. When this happens, God will give us what we ask for or what He knows to be best for us. When we use the Bible as our example to help us pray, we are being strategic in our prayer life. Joshua 1:8 states, "This Book of the Law shall not depart from your mouth, but you shall meditate in it day and night…then you will make your way prosperous, and...will have good success."

To pray effectively, we must base our prayers– as well as our spiritual growth—on God's Word. According to 19th century evangelist, George Müeller: "The vigor of our spiritual life will be in exact proportion to the place held by the Bible in our life and thoughts." Müeller has a place in the annals of Christian history as director of the Ashley Down Orphanage in Bristol, England, where he took care of thousands of children by faith and prayer. Müeller said that constant reading and meditation on God's Word strengthens our faith in God:

> Through reading of the Word of God—and especially through meditation on the Word of God—the believer becomes more and more acquainted with the nature and character of God. (The believer) sees more and more—besides His holiness and justice—what a kind, loving, gracious, merciful, mighty, wise, and faithful Being He is. [5]

The believer's trust in God deepens after reading about God's willingness to help and deliver His people, according to Müeller:

> The reading of the Word of God, together with meditation on it, will be one special means to strengthen our faith. [6]

Not only does the Word strengthen our faith, it also strengthens our prayers. For instance, if we are praying for protection, we can find scriptures in the Bible that refer to God's promise to protect His people. Psalm 91 is a perfect example because it contains verses referring to God's protection. Let's look at Psalm 91:11-12 (NLT) which says, "For he will order his angels to protect you wherever you go. They will hold you up with their hands so you won't even hurt your foot on a stone." Now, we can take these scriptures and pray, "Thank you for your protection, Lord. You said in Psalm 91:11-12 that You will order Your angels to protect me wherever I go. Your angels will hold me up with their hands so that I won't even hurt my foot on a stone."

When we use God's Word, we are praying with Divine power. Hebrews 4:12 (NIV) says, "For the word of God is alive and powerful. It is sharper than the sharpest two-edged sword, cutting between soul and spirit, between joint and marrow. It exposes our innermost thoughts and desires."

Additionally, we can use God's Word to guide our steps and as a spiritual weapon against the enemy. For example, Jesus Christ used Old Testament scripture as His spiritual weapon when He was in the wilderness being tempted by the devil as recorded in Matthew 4:1-4. When Jesus responded to Satan's temptations, He first stated, "It is written" and then repeated the scriptures. Also, Acts 2 shows how the apostle Peter used scriptures from the Old Testament to explain the promise of the outpouring of the Holy Spirit to the crowd in the Upper Room at Pentecost.

At the beginning of each chapter in this book are scripture references that relate to the type of prayer discussed in the chapter and scriptures that you can use in prayer during the prayer watches. Using Bible scripture in our prayers, however, will not guarantee that God will give us what we ask for because He doesn't always give us what we want, but what is best for us and everyone else involved. For instance, if we are praying for a person to avoid a certain situation, God may allow that person to go through the situation so that the person can build character or deepen his or her relationship with Him. So, God is actually answering our prayers but in the way that we did not expect. The Lord declares in Isaiah 55:8, "For my thoughts are not your thoughts, neither are your ways my ways…" So, we must place our faith in Him and ask that His will be done in the situation for which we are praying or in the life of the person for whom we are praying.

There are several types of prayers in God's Word and each has a specific purpose. Because of this, it is important for us to know which type of prayer to pray for our particular situation and to be aware of the best time to pray these prayers. Therefore, it is our hope that this book will motivate you to ask the Holy Spirit to help you pray effectively as you become more familiar with the eight prayer watches. We also hope that you will become aware of the most strategic times in which to pray for God's will to be done in your life and in the lives of others.

Intercessory Prayer

Related Scriptures

Genesis 18:23-33; Numbers 12:13, 14:13-19; 2 Samuel 24: 17; Daniel 9:1-19; Luke 22:32; Acts 12:5; Philippians 1:4; 1 Timothy 2:1-4; James 5:14-18

Scriptures to Use in Prayer

1 Kings 8:28; Nehemiah 1:4-6, 10-11; Psalm 17:1, 88:2; Ephesians 6:18; John 14:13-14, 15:7; James 5:16

Strategic Times to Pray

Throughout All Prayer Watches

Chapter One

Intercessory prayers can be made for anyone, for any reason, and at any time of the day or night. To "intercede" means to advocate for someone or to come before God on someone else's behalf. Intercessory prayer, then, is the act of pleading with God on behalf of those in need. So, all believers of Jesus Christ should consider themselves intercessors because "The Bible" tells us in James 5:16 to pray for each other. Author Tony M. Anderson says, "No man can be a faithful follower of Christ and not recognize his responsibility to pray for others."[1]

The Bible says in Ezekiel 22:30 that God searches for intercessors: "So I sought for a man among them who would make a wall, and stand in the gap before Me on behalf of the land, that I should not destroy it; but I found no one." In biblical times, cities were surrounded by walls which protected citizens against enemy invaders. Any type of breach in the walls had to be repaired immediately because invaders could further widen the existing gaps to gain entry into the city and attack its citizens. In the same way, Christians are called to "stand in the gap" or act as bricks that strengthen a wall with holes. By interceding and acting as a "go-between," we are making sure that the walls of divine protection for our family, friends, strangers, churches, cities, and even nations remain solid and resistant to satanic attacks.

Intercessory Prayer Leads to Spiritual Revivals

Research any revival around the world and you will find that intercessory prayer kindled the fire for a spiritual awakening. One example of this is the story of the Moravian Church that dates back to 18th century Europe. Christians from Moravia (near present day Czech Republic in Central Europe) fled to Herrnhut, a small town in the region of Saxony, Germany to escape religious persecution. Over time, the exiles began to meet on a regular basis to pray for revival.

God began to bless the Moravian community and on August 27, 1727, some of the members dedicated themselves to spend one hour each day in intercessory prayer. Other members soon joined them and a system of hourly intercessory prayer was established. After a while, community leaders dubbed the town of Herrnhut as "the Watch of the Lord." In his book, *A History of the Moravian Church*, J.E. Hutton writes:

> As the fire on the altar in the Jewish Temple was never allowed to go out (Leviticus 6:13), so the Brethren resolved that in this new

> temple of the Lord, the incense of intercessory prayer should rise continually day and night...Of all the prayer unions ever organized, surely this was one of the most remarkable. It is said to have lasted without interruption for over a hundred years.[2]

By the 1730s, the Moravians launched foreign missions projects. Members of their community traveled across land and sea to preach the gospel of Jesus Christ. Church historians believe that the Moravians influenced the 18th century's revivals in England and America. The Moravians' Christ-centered heritage of intercessory prayer lives on in Moravian Falls, North Carolina, where many Christian ministries are located to this day.

Asbury College (now named Asbury University), in Wilmore, Kentucky, has been known throughout history for its great revivals that were birthed through prevailing prayer and intercession. On several occasions the move of the Holy Spirit was so strong, it swept through the campus and reached across the nation. Tony M. Anderson was a teacher at Asbury College when spontaneous revival broke out in 1950. Anderson says:

> People came hundreds of miles to receive spiritual help. Perhaps more than five thousand people were directly influenced by this glorious spiritual awakening born in the hours of intercessory prayer.[3]

Moses, the Intercessor

The Bible shows us how Moses' intercession saved the newly formed Israeli nation from total destruction during their wilderness journey. God had miraculously set the Israelites free from slavery in Egypt, but they defied His commandments on several occasions while traveling to the land that God had promised they would inhabit.

The 14th chapter of the book of Numbers records Israel's refusal to enter their Promised Land after listening to the negative report of the spies who were sent to survey the land (Numbers 13:26-29). Of the 12 spies, 10 did not believe that Israel was strong enough to take over the land of Canaan. However, the other two spies, Joshua and Caleb, believed that Israel could conquer the land as God had promised (Numbers 13:30; 14:6). As a result of Israel's disbelief in God's promises and His ability to help them conquer the land, God threatened to disinherit Israel:

> And the Lord said to Moses, 'How long will these people treat me with contempt? Will they never believe me, even after all the miraculous signs I have done among them? I will disown them and destroy them with a plague. Then I will make you into a nation greater and mightier than they are!' (Numbers 14:11-12, NLT)

Sensing that God would carry out His plan to destroy the Israelites, Moses immediately began to intercede and ask for God's forgiveness: "In keeping with your magnificent, unfailing love, please pardon the sins of this people, just as you have forgiven them ever since they left Egypt"(Numbers 14:19, NLT). Just as Moses' intercession saved Israel, God calls on us to intercede on behalf of people and nations.

Nehemiah's Intercession for Israel

We also see intercessory prayer carried out in several passages in the book of Nehemiah. The Israelites had been exiled from Jerusalem nearly 70 years following the destruction of their city by King Nebuchadnezzar of Babylon. Years later, Cyrus, the Persian King, issued an order for the Jews to return to Jerusalem to rebuild the city and the wall (Isaiah 44:28). However, the job had not been completed during the time of Nehemiah, who served as a cupbearer to the Persian King, Artaxerxes I (Nehemiah 1:11). King Artaxerxes had previously commanded Israel to stop rebuilding Jerusalem because of the accusations Israel's enemies made against them (Ezra 4:17-24).

One of Nehemiah's brothers, Hanani, and some other men from Judah, came to visit Nehemiah. He asked them about the Jews who had escaped captivity and still live in Judah and he also asked about the city of Jerusalem, "And they said to me, 'The survivors who are left from the captivity in the province are here in great distress and reproach. The wall of Jerusalem is also broken down, and its gates are burned with fire'" (Nehemiah 1:3). After hearing the poor state of affairs of the remnant in Jerusalem, Nehemiah "sat down and wept, and mourned for many days" (Nehemiah 1:4). What Nehemiah did following this serves as an example for us in how to effectively pray an intercessory prayer. Nehemiah did the following:

- **Approached God in reverence.** Nehemiah began his prayer with reverence to God, acknowledging who He is, "...Lord God of heaven, O great and awesome God, You who keep Your covenant and mercy and those who love You and observe Your commandments" (Nehemiah 1:5).

- **Identified himself with others.** Nehemiah did not separate himself from the people. He asked God to forgive the sins of Israel and included the sins of his ancestors in his confession, "...Both my father's house and I have sinned. We have acted very corruptly against You, and have not kept the commandments, the statutes, nor the ordinances which You commanded Your servant Moses" (Nehemiah 1:6-7).

- **Reminded God of His promises to His people.** Nehemiah reminded God of His Word to Moses about what would happen when Israel sinned and how God would bring them back to their land when they repented and returned to Him (Nehemiah 1:8-9).

- **Asked God for favor and mercy.** Nehemiah asked the Lord to hear his prayer and grant him favor so King Artaxerxes would reverse his decision and allow the Israelites to rebuild Jerusalem. Nehemiah also needed favor from the king to temporarily leave his job as the king's cupbearer and lead the wall-building project (Nehemiah 2:1-8).

As we continue reading the book of Nehemiah, we see where God granted Nehemiah's intercessory prayer. Most amazingly, the wall of Jerusalem was rebuilt in 52 days and Nehemiah served as governor of Judah for 12 years (Nehemiah 5: 14; 6:15).

Jesus Christ, Our Intercessor

There cannot be a discussion on intercessory prayer without mentioning Jesus Christ, our Great High Priest, Who sits at the right hand of God and intercedes for us (Romans 8: 34). Also, Romans 8: 26-27 (ESV) tells us that we have another Heavenly Intercessor—the Holy Spirit, Who intercedes for us "with groanings too deep for words." the Gospels—the first four books of the New Testament—tells us how Jesus would rise up early in the morning to pray or spend all night in prayer. In His great intercessory prayer found in John 17, Jesus prayed for Himself, His disciples and for Believers yet to come (which is us!):

> I pray for them. I am not praying for the world, but for those you have given me, for they are yours. All I have is yours, and all you have is mine. And glory has come to me through them… My prayer is not for them alone. I pray also for those who will believe in me through their message, that all of them may be one, Father, just as you are in me and I am in you. May they also be in us so that the world may believe that you have sent me (John 17: 9-10; 20-21, NIV).

Jesus Christ always prayed effective prayers because He sought His Father's will in all that He did on earth and showed God's love for His people.

How to be Effective in Intercessory Prayer

We can learn how to effectively intercede for others from examples we find in the Bible. The following are steps we can take to do this:

1. Approach God in reverence and respect with the knowledge that He is the Only One Who can answer our prayer.

2. Ask the Holy Spirit to show us anything that we need to confess, including our sins or the sins the person for whom we are interceding (should the Holy Spirit reveal them to us).

3. Have compassion for the people for whom we are praying. Place ourselves in their position in order to understand what they may be going through.

4. Remind God of His promises. We can find what God's Word says regarding the issue for which we are interceding. For example, if we are praying for someone's healing, we can search through the Bible for scriptures on healing and incorporate them in our prayers on behalf of the sick. By doing this, we are reminding God of what He has promised in His Word about healing.

5. Ask God to show mercy and favor to the people for whom we are interceding.

Intercession can be done around the clock and until your prayer is answered. Whether you want to see a friend's need met or a spiritual awakening around the globe, it all starts with intercessory prayer, "Now this is the confidence that we have in Him, that, if we ask anything according to His will, He hears us. And if we know that He hears us, whatever we ask, we know that we have the petitions that we have asked of Him" (1 John 5:14, 15).

Sample Intercessory Prayer

Father, in the Name of Jesus, I intercede on behalf of _____. I ask for Your intervention in this situation about _____ and that you move on this person's behalf.

Thank You, Father for showing Your grace, mercy, and favor in this situation. And, as always, Lord, let Your will be done so everyone may know that You alone changed this situation, and You alone deserve all the glory. In Jesus' Name, Amen.

2. Ask the Holy Spirit to show us anything that we need to confess, including our sins or the sins the person for whom we are interceding (should the Holy Spirit reveal them to us).

3. Have compassion for the people for whom we are praying. Place ourselves in their position in order to understand what they may be going through.

4. Remind God of His promises. We can find what God's Word says regarding the issue for which we are interceding. For example, if we are praying for someone's healing, we can search through the Bible for scriptures on healing and incorporate them in our prayers on behalf of the sick. By doing this, we are reminding God of what He has promised in His Word about healing.

5. Ask God to show mercy and favor to the people for whom we are interceding.

Intercession can be done around the clock and until your prayer is answered. Whether you want to see a friend's need met or a spiritual awakening around the globe, it all starts with intercessory prayer, "Now this is the confidence that we have in Him, that, if we ask anything according to His will, He hears us. And if we know that He hears us, whatever we ask, we know that we have the petitions that we have asked of Him" (1 John 5:14, 15).

Sample Intercessory Prayer

Father, in the Name of Jesus, I intercede on behalf of _____. I ask for Your intervention in this situation about _____ and that you move on this person's behalf.

Thank You, Father for showing Your grace, mercy, and favor in this situation. And, as always, Lord, let Your will be done so everyone may know that You alone changed this situation, and You alone deserve all the glory. In Jesus' Name, Amen.

Prayer for Healing

Related Scriptures

2 Kings 20:5; Psalm 107:20; Jeremiah 30: 17a; Mark 1:32; Luke 4:40

Scriptures to Use in Prayer

Exodus 15: 26; Psalm 103:1-5; Isaiah 53:5; Jeremiah 17:14; Matthew 8:17; Galatians 3:13; James 5:15

Strategic Times to Pray

First Watch
6:00 p.m. – 9:00 p.m.

Second Watch
9:00 p.m. – 12:00 midnight

Chapter Two

The first and second prayer watches are the beginning of the night watches. This is a crucial time to pray for people who are experiencing physical sickness, emotional distress or other hardships.

The night hours can be a very lonely, depressing, and frustrating time for people, even if they are surrounded by others. While we can pray for a person's healing any time during the 24-hour prayer cycle, praying during the night hours is especially important because of the anguish people seem to feel at night.

Healing was a prominent part of the ministry of Jesus Christ, the Great Physician (Acts 10:38). Matthew 4:23 tells us that Jesus' ministry included teaching in the synagogues, preaching the gospel, and healing "all kinds of sickness and all kinds of disease among the people." The primary reasons Jesus healed the sick were to fulfill Isaiah 53:4 and to show that He has divine power to forgive sins (Matthew 8:17, 9:6). Healing the sick was so important that Jesus even healed, at times, on the Sabbath Day, which was a required day of rest for the Jewish people. Consequently, Jesus was criticized by the Jewish religious leaders for doing so (Luke 13:11-15; John 5:1-16). Also, Mark 1:32 and Luke 4:40 both point out that there were times when sick and infirmed people, and those who were possessed with demons, were brought to Jesus for healing in the evening, after the Sabbath Day was over.

Just as it is important for us to pray in faith, it is also important for the person who wants to be healed to have faith in the Healer, Jesus Christ. Jesus often took note of the faith of those who came to Him for healing. In one instance, a woman who had suffered from a blood-related illness for 12 years, pressed through a crowd of people surrounding Jesus to touch the fringe of His robe. Realizing that divine power had gone out from Him, Jesus turned to the crowd and asked, "Who touched My clothes?" (Mark 5:30). The woman reluctantly admitted what she had done. Jesus, seeing that the woman had faith in Him, said to her, "Daughter, your faith has made you well. Go in peace, and be healed of your affliction" (Mark 5:34).

According to author Alfred Edersheim, Jesus Christ, because of His great mercy and faithfulness, does not disappoint those who have strong faith in Him, like the woman healed of her blood-related infirmity. In his book, *Life and Times of Jesus the Messiah*, Edersheim writes:

> The woman learned that it was not from the garment, but from the Savior that the power proceeded; she learned also, that it was not the touch of it, but the faith in Him, that made (her) whole, and such faith must ever be (a pat) of (our) personal dealing with Him.[1]

Scriptures show us that healing is linked with faith. Jesus said if we had faith as a tiny mustard seed, we could speak to a mountain, a symbol of physical sickness or any major problem that we face, and tell it to move (Matthew 17: 20). In other words, Jesus is saying that it is not the "size" of one's faith that matters, but the "kind" of faith that places all trust in God.

Doubts and Fears in the Night

It is not unusual for people suffering from a physical illness or emotional pain to struggle with doubts about whether God actually cares for them. When we pray for the sick during the night watches, we can ask God to give them a "song in the night," which is a song of praise to God in times of sickness and trial. According to the "Prince of Preachers," Charles H. Spurgeon, all Christians will have to go through some type of "night," but they can sing about the morning to come. Spurgeon says:

> And we have many a night—nights of sorrow, nights of persecution, nights of doubt, nights of bewilderment, nights of anxiety, nights of oppression, nights of ignorance—nights of all kinds which press upon our spirits and terrify our souls. But, blessed be God, the Christian can say, "My God gives me songs in the night."… Let us go on, therefore; and if the

night is very dark, remember there is not a night that will not have a morning; and that morning is to come soon.[2]

In the midst of our doubts, we may also struggle with our fears. This is what happened to Dodie Osteen, wife of the late John Osteen, founder of Lakewood Church in Houston, Texas, and mother of Joel Osteen, the current pastor of Lakewood. Dodie Osteen said after she was diagnosed with liver cancer in the 1980s, the hardest part for her was facing her fear and believing God's Word. Osteen said:

> It wasn't my heart as much as it was my head that struggled…I knew Jesus would heal me. But in the middle of the night, the devil would say, "Well, you say you're healed, but what are you going to wear to the funeral?" And so I had to fight, but I'm telling you Jesus healed me.[3]

Dodie Osteen went on to say that she took the Word of God, made a list of scriptures pertaining to healing, and spoke them over herself until she was healed:

> Those scriptures have just been medicine to me. I take them every day and don't leave home with-out them.[4]

Thomas A. Dorsey, former jazz musician turned gospel singer and songwriter, noted how the peace of God healed him after both his wife and newborn son died the same night. It was in August 1932 when Dorsey, who lived with his wife in Chicago, Illinois, was asked to sing at a revival meeting in St. Louis, Missouri. Dorsey said he did not know why, but he was reluctant to leave his wife who was expecting their first child. But, because he was the featured soloist, he went to St. Louis.

On the second night of the revival, Dorsey received a telegraph telling him that his wife had died. Upon his return home, he found out that his newborn son had died, also. Understandably, Dorsey said he "fell apart" and even became upset with God. The following Saturday evening, Dorsey said a friend of his took him to the neighborhood music school. Dorsey recalled:

> It was quiet; the late evening sun crept through the curtained windows. I sat down at the piano, and my hands began to browse over the keys. Something happened to me, then I felt at peace. I felt as though I could reach out and touch God. I found myself playing a melody, one I'd never heard or played before, and the words (that came) into my head—they just seemed to fall into place.[5]

The song that Dorsey composed was, "Precious Lord, Take My Hand," which has since been translated into many languages and recorded by both successful gospel and secular musicians. Dorsey went on to say:

The Lord gave me these words and melody. He also healed my spirit. I learned that the Lord gave me these words and melody. He also healed my spirit. I learned that when we are in our deepest grief, when we feel farthest from God, this is when He is closest, and when we are most open to His restoring power.[6]

Healing may not come when we want it to or in the way we think it will come. But, we can be assured that God wants His people healed. And, if we press into our healing like the woman who had the issue of blood, we can receive the healing that Jesus Christ provided for us on Calvary's cross.

How to Effectively Pray for Healing

If you are praying for healing, you must first believe that God "can" and "wants" to heal you or the person for whom you are praying. One of the many names of God is "Jehovah-Rapha," which means, "The Lord Who Heals" (Exodus 15:26). So, based on God's name and His Word, there is no doubt God wants to heal us, physically, mentally, and emotionally.

There is no better way of praying effectively than praying according to the Word of God. The Epistle of James, in the New Testament, provides a guide for Christians to follow when sick people ask for prayer and when others pray for the sick. James encourages the sick to do the following:

1. **Call for the elders.** The apostle James tells those who are sick to notify the "elders of the church" (5:14). The word, "elder" is not only a title of someone holding a position in a local church, it also means someone "advanced in life" or an older adult who has gone through their own personal struggles with God's help. James does not want the sick person to face the illness alone. So, the apostle recommends that the sick call mature believers to pray for them. James also says the elders should anoint the sick with oil in the name of the Lord. In those days, oil was commonly used as a means for healing. The Good Samaritan applied oil to the man who had been beaten and robbed by thieves, according to the parable Jesus told in Luke 10:30-35. Mark 6:13 says that Jesus' disciples also anointed the sick with oil and the sick were healed.

2. **Pray with faith in God.** Faith in God, and not in ourselves or our prayers, motivates us to believe that The Great Physician, Jesus Christ, has power to heal and desires to heal the sick individual. James 5:15 (NIV) says, "And the prayer offered in faith will make the sick person well; the Lord will raise them up." James said the prayer of faith "saves" or "delivers" the sick. The Lord steps in when faith is present (Mark 5:34).

3. **Confess your sins and receive God's forgiveness.** Apparently, the apostle James saw a connection between sin and sickness: "And the prayer offered in faith will make the sick person well; the Lord will raise them up. If they have sinned, they will be forgiven. Therefore, confess your sins to each other and pray for each other so that you may be healed" (James 5:15-16, NIV). This scripture, however, does not give us license to accuse a sick person of committing sin or hiding secret sins. Job's three friends accused him of being sick because of committing some type of secret sin. James does not say that sin always causes sickness. James uses the words, "if they have sinned..." to make sure that those who are sick do not have anything blocking them from being healed.

Prayers for healing do not have to be long and complex. Simply ask God to heal you or the other person and believe that He will answer. James 5:16 says, "The effective fervent prayer of a righteous man avails much" James 5:16. To be truthful, this is easier said than done, particularly when an illness lingers. Nonetheless, we must remain steadfast and ask the Holy Spirit to help us pray with persistence until our prayer for healing is answered.

When it comes to healing, we must always remember what Jesus Christ did for us on the cross of Calvary. Jesus' death not only frees us from sin, it makes us righteous before God and provides healing for us, too. 1 Peter 2:24 (NLT) tells us, "He personally carried our sins in his body on the cross so that we can be dead to sin and live for what is right. By his wounds you are healed." As a result, we can pray effectively and powerfully for healing.

Sample Prayer for Healing

Father, I come to You in Jesus' Name, asking You to heal me (<u>or name of person</u>). Your Word says that Jesus Christ took my (<u>or name of person</u>) sins and infirmities on the cross and by His stripes I am healed. Therefore, I ask You as Jeremiah did in Jeremiah 17:14, "Heal me, Lord, and I shall be healed." Keep my heart and mind in the peace of my Lord, Jesus Christ as I await my healing. Jesus Christ healed those in need of healing, and now, I (<u>or name of person</u>) am one of them. I believe by faith in Your Word and in the power of the Blood of Jesus Christ that I (<u>or name of person</u>) am healed. All praise, honor, and glory goes to you. In Jesus' Name, Amen.

Prayer of Thanksgiving

Related Scriptures

1 Chronicles 16:34; Psalm 92:1; Psalm 119:62;
Ephesians 5:20; Philippians 4:6;
1 Thessalonians 5:18; Hebrews 13:15

Scriptures to Use in Prayer

Psalm 69:30, 75:1, 100:4-5; 2 Corinthians 2:14

Strategic Times to Pray

First Watch
6:00 p.m. – 9:00 p.m.

Fourth Watch
3:00 a.m. – 6:00 a.m.

Chapter Three

Any time is a good time to give thanks unto the Lord. The writer of Psalm 92:1 says, in part, "It is good to give thanks to the Lord." King David, "the sweet psalmist of Israel," wrote that we should give thanks to the Lord because He is good and His mercy lasts forever (Psalm 118:1).

The first prayer watch marks the end of the day. Evening time allows us to reflect on the day and thank God for being with us, regardless of what occurred. A prayer of thanksgiving helps us to shake off the offenses, annoyances, and hurts that we encountered earlier in the day and turn them over to God. Prayers of thanksgiving build our confidence in God after rehearsing to Him how great He is and how He brought us through the day. It also builds our faith to believe that He will continue to watch over us and answer our prayers.

The scriptures sometimes refer to thanksgiving as a "sacrifice" because of the difficulty we have, at times, giving thanks to God when we have encountered problems during the day. It takes an act of our will to push through and offer a "sacrifice of thanksgiving" to God.

In Psalm 116:17, the psalmist offers thanksgiving to God for delivering him out of trouble. One thing the psalmist said he would do is offer a "sacrifice of thanksgiving and call on the name of the Lord." Thanksgiving offerings were included in the sacrificial system God established for the ancient Israelites after He freed them from slavery in Egypt (Leviticus 1).

The "peace offering," also known as a "sacrifice of thanksgiving," was once considered the most joyous of all sacrifices because it expressed praise to God (Leviticus 3:1-17; 7:11-36). The person offering the sacrifice would typically invite guests to a communal meal that expressed thanksgiving to God for His mercies. This was also the only sacrifice that the offerers were allowed to share with the priests.

The fourth prayer watch is the time when the night ends and the early morning hours begin. Many believers are able to rise early, begin their devotions, and thank God for His love and mercy toward us. The prophet, Jeremiah, expressed it aptly when he said in Lamentations 3:22-23 (NIV) that, "The faithful love of the Lord never ends, His mercies never cease. Great is his faithfulness; his mercies begin afresh each morning." During our early morning prayer, we can thank God, in advance, for all the blessings He plans to bestow on us that day.

Thanksgiving, Praise, and Worship

No matter what day or night watch we choose to pray, giving thanks to God should be the first step we take when approaching Him in prayer. Psalm 100:4-5 instructs us to "enter His gates with thanksgiving and His courts with praise." The "gates" are symbolic of heaven's courts which give us access to God's heavenly throne room. Additionally, Psalm 95:2 encourages believers to come before God with thanksgiving and "shout joyfully to Him with psalms."

According to author Edward M. Bounds, thanksgiving is just what the word itself signifies—the giving of thanks to God. In his book, *Essentials of Prayer*, Bounds writes:

> Thanksgiving is giving something to God in words that we feel in our heart for blessings we've received. Gratitude arises from a contemplation of the goodness of God… (and) on what God has done for us. Both gratitude and thanksgiving point to—and have to do with—God and His mercies.[1]

Scripture shows that the prayer of thanksgiving is accompanied by praise and worship. Praise increases our faith in God as we proclaim His strength, power, and goodness toward us. According to Bounds, prayer, praise, and thanksgiving are closely associated:

> Praise and thanksgiving are so near alike that it is not easy to distinguish between them or define them separately…The Psalms are filled with many songs of praise and hymns of thanksgiving, all pointing back to the results of prayer.[2]

When we praise God, we are exalting Him for Who He is and What He has done. In Psalm 18:1-3, for example, David described the Lord as his "refuge," "shield," "fortress," "strength," and "deliverer." We see that David was exalting God for Who He is and what God had done for him. And, David acknowledged that God was worthy of praise because He saved David from his enemies.

With worship, we hold God in reverence, respect, and honor for His greatness and awesomeness, and this humbles us in the process. Psalm 95:6-7 encourages us to "worship," "bow down," and "kneel" before the Lord, our Creator, "for He is our God…" All of these actions describe the physical expression of submission to God. When we worship God, in a sense, we are saying about God what John the Baptist said about Jesus Christ the Messiah: "He must increase but I must decrease."

How to Effectively Pray a Prayer of Thanksgiving

To pray effectively during the first and fourth prayer watches, we simply recall all that God has done for us and our loved ones and thank Him for His grace, love, and mercy.

There are times when thanksgiving, praise, and worship arise spontaneously from our hearts. Among the best examples in the Bible of spontaneous praise is found in

1 Samuel 2:1-10 when Hannah praised the Lord for blessing her with her first-born son, Samuel. Hannah had not been able to have children, but she prayed a prayer of petition asking the Lord to bless her to give birth to a boy (1 Samuel 1:11). The next example is similar to Hannah's prayer and is found in Luke 1:46-55. In these verses, Mary praises and worships the Lord after the angel, Gabriel revealed to her that she would give birth to Jesus Christ, the Messiah.

Sample Morning Prayer of Thanksgiving

Father, in the Name of Jesus, thank You for watching over me during the night and waking me to see another day. I bless You, and glorify You, and worship You, for You alone are worthy of praise. I surrender myself to you this morning. Help me not to yield to temptation and rescue me from the traps set for me by the Evil One.

Thank you for Your faithfulness and Your tender mercies that are new every morning. Father, I ask that You go before me and prepare my way, in Jesus' Name, Amen.

Sample Evening Prayer of Thanksgiving

Father, in the Name of Jesus, thank You for walking with me through the day. Father, You did not leave my side for one moment, even when I felt overwhelmed in different situations.

Father, at the end of the day, I ask for Your forgiveness for anything that I said, anything that I did, or anything that I thought that was not pleasing to You and showed disrespect to others.

I praise and thank You for Your love, care, mercy, and goodness to me, in Jesus' Name, Amen.

Prayer of Petition

Related Scriptures

2 Chronicles 6:21, Psalm 20: 5; Daniel 9:3; John 14:13-14; Philippians 4:6; 1 Timothy 2:1, 5:5; 2 Timothy 1:3; James 1:5-6; 1 John 5:15

Scriptures to Use in Prayer

2 Chronicles 6:39; Psalm 28:2; Psalm 143:1

Strategic Times to Pray

Throughout All Watches

Chapter Four

A petition is a formal request to an authority for a cause or a need. When we petition God in prayer, we are asking God, our Heavenly Authority, to do something on our behalf that we cannot do for ourselves. Petition prayers are usually prayed repeatedly until we receive an answer from God. The person petitioning God is, in essence, saying, "I am not going to give up or stop praying until I have the assurance that my prayer has been answered." If we pray according to God's will, we can be certain that He will answer our petitions in His own time and in His own way.

While we can petition God at any time, prayers of petition are often prayed during the night watches because there is something about the darkness that causes our imaginations to stir up anxiety and fears of all kind. In the Old Testament book of Lamentations, the Prophet Jeremiah mourned over the destruction of Jerusalem. Jeremiah and other prophets, whom God called His "watchmen" (Jeremiah 6:6), prophesied against the sins of the nation of Judah, but the people ignored their warnings. As a result, the Babylonians destroyed Jerusalem and burned the Temple (2 Kings 25). Jeremiah found the devastation hard to handle, especially at night, and the prophet urged other distressed survivors to lift their voices and cry out to God:

> Arise, cry out in the night as the watches of the night begin; pour out your heart like water in the presence of the Lord. Lift up your hands to him for the lives of your children, who faint from hunger at every street corner (Lamentations 2:19, NIV).

Night is also a time when our needs and the needs of others are the most apparent. In Luke 11:5-10, Jesus Christ told a parable about a man who came to his friend's house at midnight and asked to borrow three loaves of bread. The man had an unexpected visitor and he did not have food to feed his guest. It was customary in that day to lodge and feed guests. So, to be without food was an insult to the guests and shameful to the host. The friend turned him down, "Do not trouble me; the door is now shut, and my children are with me in bed; I cannot rise and give to you" (Luke 11:7). The man, however, was insistent in his petition and refused to leave his friend's house empty-handed. Jesus said the friend finally got up and gave the man bread, not because the man was his friend, but because of the man's persistence. In telling this parable, Jesus was urging His disciples to be persistent when petitioning God in prayer.

In the Bible, a prayer of petition is also called a "prayer of importunity." The simplest definition for "importunity," is an "insistence that rises to shamelessness," according to the *International Standard Bible Encyclopedia*.[1] The shamelessness does not come so much in the way a person acts outwardly, but in the sense that a person is not ashamed to persevere in prayer until the answer comes.

Jesus says that if we continue to persist in our prayers, we would be rewarded with the answer:

> So I say to you, ask, and it will be given to you; seek, and you will find; knock, and it will be opened to you. For everyone who asks receives, and he who seeks finds, and to him who knocks it will be opened" (Luke 11:9-10).

When we persist in our prayers of petition, it will soon become apparent to others that we are determined to obtain the things that we seek, like the man in the parable who asked for three loaves of bread. Author Tony M. Anderson believes this parable shows that people know who to contact when they need prayer:

> The news that a certain person can prevail with God in prayer will soon reach a multitude of hopeless and helpless people. Some distressed soul will soon be knocking at that (person's) door seeking help and comfort.[2]

Prayers of petition are most effective when God lays a burden on your heart about something you are in need of or when someone else is in need of God's intervention. Being persistent in petitioning prayer does not mean that we are begging God to intervene, but rather we are reminding God that there is nothing too difficult for Him because He is Almighty and the Only One who can resolve this issue.

A Prayer of Petition is Spirit Led

As with all other forms of prayer, a prayer of petition is led by the Holy Spirit, based on God's Word, and on a solid faith that God will answer in His own way and in His own time, and for His glory. There will be times when we know the will of God for the matter for which we are praying, and we can pray that His will takes precedence. However, there will be times when we are not sure of God's will, and we have to ask the Holy Spirit to help us pray.

Rees Howells, one of the most famous intercessors in modern Christian history, was director of the Bible College of Wales during the dark days of World War II. From 1936 until the end of the war in 1945, Howells and his students, as well as other intercessors, would meet from 7:00 p.m. to 12:00 midnight (first and second prayer watches) and sometimes during the day, to petition God for victory over the Germans.

According to documents written during that era, there were times when Howells and the intercessors did not know what matters to pray about, but Howells credited the Holy Spirit for showing them what events were about to take place and how to pray more effectively about them.

One event for which the intercessors petitioned God was the rescue of over 300,000 British, French, and Belgium soldiers who were trapped on the beaches of Dunkirk, France, as German forces advanced. Not only did Rees Howells and his intercessors petition God, but also Britain's King, George VI called for a National Day of Prayer. The evacuation of the Allied troops, from May 26, 1940 to June 4, 1940, has gone down in history as the "Miracle of Dunkirk."[3]

As we are led by the Spirit and persist in prayer, our faith in God increases, as does our spiritual growth and confidence in God. The apostle John says that once we have confidence in God, and if we ask anything according to His will, we know that He will grant our petition, "And if we know that he hears us, whatever we ask, we know that we have the petitions that we have asked of him" (1 John 5:14-15).

How to Effectively Pray a Prayer of Petition

There are several elements involved in praying an effective prayer of petition. The most important are the following:

- **Determination.** Like the man in the parable who needed bread, we must have our minds made up and resolute in getting an answer.

- **Perseverance.** We must refuse to give up until we receive an answer.

- **Intensity.** We must pray with boldness, passion, and what may look to others like shamelessness before God.

In addition, it is most important to ask God for His will to be done in whatever issue we are bringing to Him. We should follow Jesus' model prayer, which asks for God's will to be done on Earth. This is actually the answer to our prayer.

Sample Prayer of Petition

Father, in the Name of Jesus, I ask for Your help in (situation in which you are praying about or for the person for whom you are praying). You are great and powerful and no one can come against You. Only You can help me or (name of person). Your Word says in Luke 10:9 to ask and what I need will be given, seek until I find what I need, and knock and You will open the door for me. So, I am doing as Your Word directs.

Holy Spirit, I ask You to show me how I should pray for (the issue or event) and lead me to other intercessors when necessary, so that we can pray corporately for Your will to be done.

I thank You, Father, for hearing me when I pray, and answering my petition, in Jesus' Name, Amen.

Prayer for God's Justice

Related Scriptures

Exodus 2:23-25; 69:13-19; Psalm 7:11;
Isaiah 59:14-19; Hebrews 6:19; Jude 14-15;
Revelation 6:9-11

Scriptures to Use in Prayer

Deuteronomy 32:3-4; Psalm 35:1-2, 89:13-14;
Jeremiah 11:20, 15:15

Strategic Times to Pray

Second Watch (Midnight Watch)
9:00 p.m. – 12:00 midnight

Third Watch (Cockcrowing Watch)
12:00 midnight – 3:00 a.m.

Chapter Five

Prayers for God's justice can be prayed during the second and third prayer watches based on scriptures showing God releasing His judgments during the night hours against those who oppose His laws and His people.

Among the most well-known passages in the Bible of God executing judgment on behalf of His people is the one found in Exodus 12:29 where God judged the Egyptians, who had enslaved the Israelites for 400 years. At midnight, God sent a plague that killed all the first-born Egyptian males and the first-born of their cattle. After the horrific deaths throughout the land, Pharaoh freed Israel from slavery.

God also judged the Assyrian army which had planned to attack Judah. In 2 Kings 19, Hezekiah asked God to intervene on Judah's behalf because the Assyrian King, Sennacherib had invaded Judah and warned King Hezekiah of his plans to attack the city of Jerusalem (2 Kings 18-19).

God answered King Hezekiah's prayer with a judgment on the Assyrians for defying and blaspheming God, "That night the angel of the Lord went out to the Assyrian camp and killed 185,000 Assyrian soldiers. When the surviving Assyrians woke up the next morning, they found corpses everywhere" (2 Kings 19:35, NLT). The Bible says in Psalm 89:14 that God's heavenly throne rests upon justice and righteousness (doing what is right). Therefore, we must ask the Holy Spirit to help us pray effectively for justice to come to people who are facing physical persecution, torture, and even death because of their ethnicity, religious or political beliefs.

Imprecatory Prayers

In the Old Testament, whenever God's people were in unjust situations or their cities had been defeated by an enemy army, they would pray what is called, "imprecatory prayers." The word, "imprecatory" means to call down or invoke judgment or a curse on one's enemies and to cry out for justice. One of the most intense examples of an imprecatory prayer is found in Revelation 6:9-11 (NIV) where end-time Christian martyrs cried out to God to take vengeance on their persecutors, "They called out in a loud voice, 'How long, Sovereign Lord, holy and true, until you judge the inhabitants of the earth and avenge our blood?'"

The Bible shows that not only do humans plead to God to avenge them, but God can apparently hear the blood of innocent murder victims crying to Him for revenge. We see an example of this with Cain and Abel, the sons of Adam and Eve. Cain was angry with his brother because God accepted Abel's sacrifice and not his (Genesis 4:3-5). So, one day while walking in a field together, Cain killed Abel, and the Lord confronted Cain about the murder, "And He (the Lord) said, 'What have you done? The voice of your brother's blood cries out to Me from the ground'"(Genesis 4:10).

Those who prayed imprecatory prayers in the Bible asked God to avenge them, they were not taking matters into their own hands by seeking personal revenge. For instance, before David became Israel's second king, he was being hunted by Saul, Israel's first king. Saul was jealous of David and wanted to kill him. David had opportunities to kill Saul but he refused. He told Saul, "Let the Lord judge between you and me, and let the Lord avenge me on you. But my hand shall not be against you" (1 Samuel 24:12).

Some Christians believe imprecatory prayers should not be prayed today because these prayers are mostly found in the Old Testament and we are no longer under the law given by Moses. Instead, we are under the New Testament which brings grace and truth through Jesus Christ (John 1:17). Therefore, we should follow Jesus Christ's command to love our enemies and do good to those who persecute us (Matthew 5: 43-48, Luke 6:27-38).

God does not approve of us calling down curses or exacting personal revenge on someone who has harmed us. However, in some circumstances, it is appropriate to ask God to execute His Divine justice against those who commit inhumane and heinous acts. In these particular situations, the Holy Spirit will show us what to pray for and how to pray. What is important to remember is not to pray according to our natural, soulish emotions, but to pray Holy Spirit-led prayers for God's will to be done in the midst of dire and unjust situations. While we may pray to God for justice, it is God alone Who renders the judgment! James 4:12, NIV tells us, "There is one Lawgiver and Judge who is able to save and destroy."

Praying for God's Justice

Jesus Christ told His disciples that God responds to prayers of justice that are prayed by His people. In Luke 18:1–6 (NLT), Jesus told a parable about a widow who went to a godless, unjust judge "who had great contempt for everyone." The widow went to appeal for justice against someone who had harmed her (vs. 3). The judge ignored the widow for a while, but she repeatedly came back to him to demand vindication from her enemy. The judge became so tired of her that he said to himself, "I don't fear God or care about people, but this woman is driving me crazy. I'm going to see that she gets justice, because she is wearing me out with her constant requests!" (vs. 4-5).

Jesus told His disciples to learn a lesson from the parable of the unjust judge, "Even he rendered a just decision in the end, so don't you think God will surely give justice to his chosen people who plead with him day and night? Will he keep putting them off? I tell you, he will grant justice to them quickly!" (vs. 7-8a). God's character is not like the unjust judge's character in the parable. God is a God Who cares about people and shows mercy, even in the midst of judgment (Habakkuk 3:1, James 2:13).

However, Jesus pointed out that God will do what is right and just "in His own time and in His own way" to vindicate His people. According to Ecclesiastes 3:17, ESV: "God will judge the righteous and the wicked, for there is a time for every matter and for every work." So, know that if you have been victimized in any way, God will avenge you. You only need to trust Him.

How to Effectively Pray for God's Justice

To pray effectively for God's justice, we should do the following:

1. State the unjust situation or issue as we see it.

2. Ask God to show us the situation from His perspective. Read Isaiah 55:8 that says God's ways are not our ways and His thoughts are not like our thoughts.

3. Pray as the Holy Spirit leads that God will impose His justice or judgment in the matter for which you are praying.

Sample Prayer for God's Justice

Father, I come before You in Jesus' Name asking that You show justice (or Your judgment) in the matter of_____. Stop me, Father from taking matters into my own hands or plotting revenge on those who have mistreated me (or others). Your Word says that vengeance is Yours and You will repay it. Your Word also says in Psalm 7 that You are a righteous Judge and You demand justice. So, I ask You to stand up on my behalf (or on behalf of others) against _____ and stop their evil actions. I thank You Father, for being my help and strength and I thank You for Your justice, in Jesus' Name, Amen.

Prayer for Protection

Related Scriptures

1 Samuel 2:9; 2 Samuel 22:3-4;
Psalm 41:2; Nahum 1:7

Scriptures to Use in Prayer

Psalm 18:2-3, 23:4, 32:7; 46:1-2, 63:6-7; 91

Strategic Times to Pray

Second Watch (Midnight Watch)
9:00 p.m. – 2:00 midnight

Third Watch (Cockcrowing)
12:00 midnight – 3:00 a.m.

Fifth Watch
6:00 a.m. – 9:00 a.m.

Seventh Watch
12:00 noon – 3:00 p.m.

Chapter Six

The second and third prayer watches are opportune times to pray God's protection over yourself, your family, your nation, and others. As things are normally hidden from view in the darkness, the night watches remind us that we are spiritually hidden in God, which Psalm 91:1-2 calls a "secret place" and "refuge:"

> He who dwells in the secret place of the Most High shall abide under the shadow of the Almighty. I will say of the Lord, "He is my refuge and my fortress; my God, in Him I will trust."

In biblical times, a fortress was a secured tower used as a military stronghold and usually located on a high cliff or mountain. Soldiers could ward off their enemies from these lofty and secured places. Something similar happens in the animal kingdom. A frequent sight in Alaska are Dall sheep. They can move about on steep, rocky cliffs with relative ease because of their hooves. Dall sheep also have large ears that help them detect sounds from all directions, while their eyes, on the sides of their heads, allow them to see in several directions at once. In the winter, the sheep move to lower terrain and their white color camouflages them in the snow from predators. However, when the sheep sense danger, they flee to the safety of higher rocks and crags where hunters or predatory animals cannot reach them.

Just as Dall sheep protect themselves by running on rugged terrain to higher altitudes, we can run to God Most High (or in Hebrew, "El Elyon"), our "spiritual" fortress for protection. The German reformer, Martin Luther, wrote a hymn titled, *A Mighty Fortress is Our God*. In the lyrics, Luther describes God as a "bulwark" (a defensive wall) that never fails. Because we find security in God, we should not be afraid of attacks from enemies—personal or otherwise—that come during the day or night. Psalm 91:5-6 describes these attacks as the "terror by night" and the "pestilence that walks in darkness" (during the second and third prayer watches); and the "arrow that flies by day" and "destruction that lays waste at noonday"(during the seventh prayer watch).

Attacks can come to us personally or in our nation's cities. For instance, America remembers the coordinated suicide attacks against the World Trade Center in New York City's financial district and the Pentagon in Washington, D.C. on September 11, 2001. However, this was not the first time New York was attacked in the daytime. In fact, the city's financial district was bombed during the seventh prayer watch more than 80 years prior to 2001! The bombing was never solved, but investigators and historians believed it was carried out due to post-World War I social unrest in the United States.[1]

God wants us to run to Him as swiftly as Dall sheep flee from their pursuers to higher levels. Through prayer, reading and meditating on the Word of God, and placing our faith in Him, we can stand firm in times of adversity and find our protection in El Elyon, the Most High God.

Praying for the Protection of Others

Not only do we ask God for protection for ourselves, there are times when God warns us to pray for the protection of others. Author Kathy S. Wilson illustrates this point very well in her book, *The Faithfulness of Our God*. Wilson told of the time when she was scheduled to pick up her son and his friend from the airport. Wilson said she was heading downstairs in her home when she heard God's voice telling her to pray for the airplane on which her son would be traveling. Wilson said God also told her to contact her son and sister (who was also her son's godmother) and tell them to pray, as well. Wilson immediately sent a text message to her son and sister and told them about the directions God had given her. Afterwards, she began to pray as God had instructed her. Wilson then moved into her seer gift (a seer in the Bible is a prophet who has visions of the future). Wilson writes:

> I could see my son's plane ascending over the clouds and a huge hand holding the entire plane in its palm. I knew this huge

hand was the hand of God. As I continued in prayer, I saw the airplane my son had boarded landing safely at the airport. I began to thank God and trusted that everything was fine.

That evening when I picked my son up from the airport, he told me that he thanked God for having a praying and obedient mother. He said the plane landed at the airport and taxied only to the beginning of the runway where it stopped because of engine trouble! The plane had to be towed to the landing gate.

Praise God! I know it was the Lord who held the plane up in the air and then safely sat it down on the ground at the airport. [2]

God's "huge hand" of protection can hold us up too, as we are obedient in carrying out His directions while remaining in the "secret place of the Most High."

Staying Sheltered Under the Blood of Jesus

We can also find protection through the Blood of Jesus. When we think of the Blood of Jesus, we immediately think of salvation—and rightly so. Through His death, burial and resurrection, Jesus Christ paid the penalty for our sins so that we might obtain God's righteousness, which means our being in right-standing with God.

However, the Blood of Jesus not only has the power to save us, it also has the power to protect us, just as the blood of a sacrificial lamb protected the Israelites from God's final plague in Egypt (Exodus 12). Before God released Israel from slavery, He told Moses to tell the people to sacrifice a lamb and put the lamb's blood on the doorposts of their homes. This would distinguish the Israelites from the Egyptians. God had previously released nine plagues on the Egyptians and the tenth and final plague (in which God would strike down every firstborn male—both human and animal) would be the most devastating one to take place before Pharaoh would give his unconditional permission for the Israelites to leave Egypt:

> For I will pass through the land of Egypt on that night, and will strike all the first-born in the land of Egypt, both man and beast; and against all the gods of Egypt I will execute judgment: I am the Lord. Now the blood shall be a sign for you on the houses where you are. And when I see the blood, I will pass over you; and the plague shall not be on you to destroy you when I strike the land of Egypt (Exodus 12:12-13).

God's protection of Israel by the blood of a lamb was symbolic of the Divine covering provided for us by the Blood of Jesus Christ. Because we have been saved by the Blood of Jesus, we are in a Blood Covenant with God. When we decree the blood of Jesus over our lives, we become victorious over the power of the Enemy. This is why we can pray each day for the Blood of Jesus to cover us, our families, our homes, and our nation from satanic attacks, accidents and other tragedies. We can also pray for the Blood of Jesus to cover our minds, hearts, and bodies when we are worried, afraid or need physical or emotional healing.

Because we live in a fallen world, the only safe place for us to be is under the Blood of Jesus. We must not take our salvation for granted and think that we are protected from tragedy just because we are saved. We can experience tragedy just like those who do not confess Jesus Christ as their Lord and Savior. Should we die, we will be with the Lord in eternity, but it is possible for us to die prematurely. This is why it is important for us to be obedient to whatever God tells us to do (or not to do), and not second-guess His Holy Spirit when He speaks to us but follow. We should follow His leading (because the Holy Spirit guides us into all truth, John 16:13) and apply the Blood of Jesus so that the enemy will not take us away from this earth before our time.

God wants us to run to Him as swiftly as Dall sheep flee from their pursuers to higher levels. Through prayer, reading and meditating on the Word of God, placing our faith in Him, and being covered with the Blood of Jesus, we can stand firm in times of adversity and find our protection in El Elyon, the Most High God.

How to Effectively Pray for Protection

To pray an effective prayer of protection, we can pray Psalm 91 each day. Also, we can pray for the Blood of Jesus to cover us, our loved ones and all that God has entrusted to us.

Sample Prayer for Protection

Father, in the Name of Jesus and by His Blood, I am grateful that my safety is in Your Presence. Because I dwell in You, and You in me, Your Word says in Psalm 91, that I can abide under the shadow of the Almighty. I will say of You, Lord, "You are my refuge and my fortress; my God, in You I will trust."

You will rescue me from my attackers—those who would try to set a trap for me— and from deadly diseases. You will cover me with Your feathers and shelter me with Your wings, just as a mother bird protects her young ones. Your truth and faithful promises are my shield and protection.

I will not be afraid of the terrors of the night, nor the arrow that files in the day, nor the disease that walks in darkness, nor the disaster that strikes at noon. A thousand may fall at my side and ten thousand at my right hand; but it shall not come near me. Only with my eyes shall I look, and see the reward of the wicked.

Because I have made You, the Most High God, my refuge and dwelling place, no evil will conquer me, nor will any plague come near my home; for You will give Your angels orders to protect me everywhere I go. They will hold me up with their hands, so I won't even hit my foot against a stone. I shall tread upon my enemies, who are like lions and cobras, and trample them under my feet.

Father, because I love You, You said that You will rescue me, and when I call on You, You will answer me. You will be with me in trouble and honor me. You will satisfy me with long life and show me Your saving power. Thank You, Lord, in Jesus' Name, Amen.

Spiritual Warfare Prayer

Related Scriptures

Deuteronomy 28:7; 2 Chronicles 20:15; Psalm 18:39

Scriptures to Use in Prayer

Matthew 18:18-19; 1 Corinthians 15:57; Ephesians 6:10-18

Strategic Prayer Time

Third Prayer Watch
12:00 midnight – 3:00 a.m.

Chapter Seven

The third prayer watch is during the most demonic part of the night because it is the time period that is most associated with supernatural events. This watch is also known as the "Witching Hour" and the "Devil's Hour." This is Satan's prime time to launch attacks into the natural realm through those over whom he has influence. While Satan has those who follow him in darkness, Jesus Christ has followers, who are called "children of light" (Ephesians 5:8). First Thessalonians 5:5 (NLT) says that Christ's followers are "all children of the light and of the day."

Although we are "children of the light," at some point in our walk of faith, we have to face Satan who attempts to overrule God's plans and purposes for our lives and the lives of our loved ones and friends. Our strategy in this war is to stand in the shadow of the Cross of Jesus Christ, cover ourselves with the Blood of Jesus, and wield the Word of God as a sword to remind Satan of his defeat at Calvary. Jesus' triumph on the cross has made us victors in Christ, and not victims of Satan.

It is important that we remember this fact when we become involved in spiritual warfare. We must know who we are in Jesus Christ and have our faith firmly rooted in Him when we encounter attacks from Satan. Scottish theologian, James Orr, writes that warfare should not come as a surprise to Christians:

> It is blessed and glorious to be a Christian...The Christian, however, does not go to heaven on flowery beds of ease. His pathway is not strewn with roses all the way; there is now and then a thorn. It is not sunshine all the time; now and then a shadow falls. To win heaven, he must fight... (Christian warfare) is a life-long struggle, and it is also a life-long victory, and in the end, eternal victory. [1]

We see in Luke 22:31, that Satan wanted to attack Peter, but Jesus interceded, just as He does for us today. Jesus told Peter that Satan "demanded to have you, that he might sift you like wheat, but I have prayed for you that your faith may not fail; and when you have turned again, strengthen your brethren." Although it appears that Jesus was only talking to Peter, the word, *you* in this verse is plural, which means Jesus was referring to the remaining 11 disciples. Satan had already entered into the heart of Judas, the disciple who betrayed Jesus (Luke 22:3-4).

Satan wants to do the same to us. Thankfully, however, Jesus Christ, our Great High Priest makes intercession for us (Hebrews 4:14; 7:25), just as He did for Peter, so that our faith in Him will not fail when Satan tries to toss us around like wheat in a sieve. Charles H. Spurgeon says that

"God grants to Satan permission to try His people in this way because God knows how He will overrule it to His own Glory and their good." [2]

Praying an Effective Spiritual Warfare Prayer

While many Believers in Christ are asleep from 12:00 midnight to 3:00 a.m., God calls some to engage in spiritual warfare during the third prayer watch. We must not be afraid of Satan, yet we must be cautious when fighting spiritual battles during this watch. We cannot devise our own "spiritual warfare plan" and think that we will be effective intercessors.

Depending on the type of spiritual warfare in which we are engaged, God may have us join with other seasoned intercessors to confront "spiritual wickedness in high places" (Ephesians 6:12). Some churches and ministries hold special prayer meetings from the second prayer watch through the fourth prayer watch (9:00 p.m. through 6:00 a.m.). These "night watchmen" mount prayer attacks against satanic activity and see God's power manifest.

Because of the occult activities that occur during this watch, the Godhead helps us to pray. God the Father guards us as we pray against the enemy, God the Son gives us the authority, through His blood, to take on the enemy, while God the Holy Spirit shows us exactly how to pray God's will against the enemy and for our lives.

As we pray, we must remember to clothe ourselves with the spiritual armor that God has given to us as detailed in Ephesians 6:10-17. The apostle Paul compared these spiritual weapons to the weapons that Roman soldiers carried in his day. This is an appropriate comparison because Paul refers to Believers in Christ as soldiers and urges them to "fight the good fight of faith" (1 Timothy 6:12). According to J.C. Ryle:

> The true Christian is called to be a soldier, and must behave as such from the day of His conversion to the day of his death. He is not meant to live a life of religious ease, indolence, and security. He must never imagine for a moment that he can sleep and doze along the way to heaven…If the Bible is the rule of his faith and practice, he will find his course laid down very plainly in this matter: He must fight.[3]

Sample Spiritual Warfare Prayer

When it comes to spiritual warfare, it is best to be led by the Holy Spirit and pray from the Holy Bible. This sample prayer is taken from Ephesians 6: 12-18:

Father, I put on the spiritual armor that You have given me so that I can resist satanic beings in the spirit world; and, having done all to stand firmly in place, I hold my ground.

I tie the belt of truth around my waist. Father, Your Word is truth.

I put on the breastplate of righteousness because I am in right standing with You, through Jesus Christ. My feet are protected in preparation to face the enemy with a firm-footed stability and readiness produced by the good news of Your redemption and love for the world.

I place the shield of faith over myself to extinguish all the fiery darts of the devil.

I put on the helmet of salvation to protect my mind from doubts and self-condemnation and to bring balance to my life.

I focus my mind on God's love and power and will not be led away from the truth.

I use the sword of the Spirit (which is alive, active and powerful) by speaking the Word of God as it applies to whatever situation I may face. I plant God's Word deep in my heart so I will always be ready to cut down lies with His truth.

I will pray in the spirit and intercede for all Christians as the Holy Spirit prompts me. I believe that the Holy Spirit is interceding on my behalf according to my prayers (Ephesians 6: 12-18).

Father, surround me with Your hedge of protection as I move forward on the spiritual battlefield today.

Prayer for Direction

Related Scriptures

Psalm 32:8, 37:23-24;
Isaiah 30:21, 48:17-18; John 16:13

Scriptures to Use in Prayer

Psalm 31:3; Psalm 119:105;
Proverbs 3:5-6; Jeremiah 33:3

Strategic Time to Pray

Fifth Prayer Watch
6:00 a.m. – 9:00 a.m.

Chapter Eight

The fifth prayer watch is the time when many people start their day. As we prepare to go through our day, it is important for us to ask God to direct us and show us what He wants us to do and where He wants us to go. By praying for God's direction, we are acknowledging God's rule over our lives.

The writer of Psalm 119:133 (NLT) asked God to guide his steps by His Word, so he would not be overcome by evil. According to Charles H. Spurgeon, this scripture is a prayer that asks the Lord to "order our ordinary daily lives." While this should be our continual prayer, some people believe this "ties us up pretty tightly" and restricts our freedom of choice. Spurgeon responds:

> No, my friend, I do not want to tie you up at all! You can roam where you like, but I know that the tighter I am tied, the better it is for me, and the happier I am. There is a prayer in the 118th Psalm which I always like to pray, "Bind the sacrifice with cords even to the horns of the altar." Lord, hold me fast from morning till night, and through the night as well! I long that You should fill my very dreams with thoughts of You! [1]

Edward M. Bounds stressed the importance of developing a habit of praying in the morning to seek God's will. In his book, *Power Through Prayer*, Bounds writes:

> The men who have done the most for God in this world have been on their knees. He who (wastes) away the early morning, its opportunity and freshness, in other pursuits than seeking God, will make poor headway seeking him the rest of the day. If God is not first in our thoughts and efforts in the morning, he will be in last place the rest of the day.[2]

So, when we pray for God's direction, we are actually consecrating ourselves and our day to God.

Consecration Keeps Us in God's Hand

The word, "consecration" means to "be set apart for use by God" or "to be set aside as holy." We find several instances in the Old Testament of how Israel's priests were consecrated so that they could minister before God and accept the sacrifices brought by the people (Exodus 30:30). Edward M. Bounds defines consecration as "a voluntary dedication or offering of ourselves to God." In his book, *Essentials of Prayer*, Bounds writes:

> It is the setting apart of all we are, all we have, and all we expect to have or be, to God first of all. It is not so much the giving of ourselves to the Church, or the mere engaging in some line of Church work. Almighty God is in view and He is the end of all consecration. Consecration has a sacred nature. It is devoted to holy ends. It is the voluntary putting of one's self in God's hands to be used sacredly, in holiness, and with sanctifying ends in view.[3]

When we consecrate ourselves, we should not be surprised when God changes our plans to carry out His will. We find an example of this in Acts 16: 6-9 during the apostle Paul's second missionary journey. Paul and Silas were devoted to preaching the gospel of Jesus Christ and relied on the Holy Spirit to direct their steps. The apostles planned to preach in the Roman province of Asia but were forbidden by the Holy Spirit to go there.

Then, the apostles wanted to go north to Bithynia, but once again, the Holy Spirit would not allow them to travel there. So, Paul and Silas went to Troas. While there, Paul had a night vision of a man who pleaded with him, saying, "Come over into Macedonia and help us" (Acts 16:9). As soon as Paul had seen the vision, he and Silas prepared to leave for Macedonia (Greece), concluding that God opened the door for them to preach the gospel of Jesus Christ in Europe, something they had not previously planned.

Sometimes when we pray for God's direction, we do not realize that God may be closing doors so that we can undertake new endeavors, like Paul and Silas. God's direction may also save our lives, just like it did for His only Son, Jesus, Who was consecrated before He came to Earth as Savior of the human race. Shortly after His birth, Jesus faced threats to His life. But, it was not God's will yet for Jesus to die for the sins of the world.

One night, Joseph, Jesus' earthly father, had a dream in which an Angel of the Lord told him to "flee into Egypt" with Jesus and his mother, Mary, because King Herod planned to slaughter all male children two years old and under (Matthew 2:16). Herod was angry because the wise men from the East had come to Bethlehem to pay homage to Jesus Christ, the new "King of the Jews," and left town—after being warned of God in a dream—without telling Herod the location of the baby king (Matthew 2:11-12). Joseph obeyed God's directions, fled to Egypt, and spared the life of his earthly son, Jesus.

Why Do We Need to Ask God for Direction?

Is it necessary for Believers in Christ to ask God for direction? And, if so, what type of direction do we ask Him for? First, if we want to make sure that we are in God's perfect will for our lives, and if we want Him to know that we trust Him with our lives, we will ask for direction. Secondly, praying for God's direction may prevent us from falling into traps that Satan has set for us. This is one of the reasons why Jesus Christ told His disciples to pray to God the Father, "And do not lead us into temptation (testings), but deliver us from the evil one" (Matthew 6:13).

Left on our own, it is easy for us to be lured into a trap of Satan. Satan loves to distract us so that we do not see temptation coming. But, when we pray for God's guidance, He will answer our prayers for direction by warning us when He sees us walking into Satan's trap. For instance, the Holy Spirit, helps us to avoid being in places we do not belong, just because we may be bored, curious or following the desires of our sinful nature. John 16:13 says, "However, when He, the Spirit of truth, has come, He will guide you into all truth."

A story is told about a wealthy merchant who was allowed access into the headquarters of Arthur Wellesley, the First Duke of Wellington, at the battle of Waterloo. Wellesley led the Anglo-Allied forces in defeating French Emperor Napoleon Bonaparte and his army at Waterloo in June 1815. Gunfire was heard all around and the merchant was concerned that Wellesley was exposing him to great danger. Wellesley told the merchant, "You have no business here, but I am performing my duty." From this story, author Newman Hall advises us not to go into spiritual danger because of "idle curiosity, but only when duty calls: then, and then alone, may we expect to be safe."[4]

How to Effectively Pray for Direction

To pray effectively, we must ask God for His guidance. When we do this, we are placing our dependence on Him. We can also ask God for His wisdom and discernment so that we will know how to make wise decisions and be certain that we are hearing God's voice.

Sample Prayer for Direction

Father, I come before You, in Jesus' Name, thanking You for blessing me with another day. Your Word in Psalm 37: 23 says, "The steps of a good man are ordered by the Lord, and He delights in his way." So, Father, I give my day to you and ask that You lead me, by Your Holy Spirit, to the places You want me to go, and stop me from going to those places You do not want me to go.

I thank You, Lord, that You are guiding me today, in Jesus Name, Amen.

Prayer for Forgiveness

Related Scriptures

Psalm 25:11; Micah 7:18-19

Scriptures to Use in Prayer

Psalm 51:1-2, Matthew 6:12; Ephesians 1:7; 1 John 1:9

Strategic Time to Pray

Seventh Prayer Watch
12:00 noon – 3:00 p.m.

Chapter Nine

The seventh prayer watch is the time Jesus Christ hung on the cross to die for the sins of all humanity. According to Matthew 27:45 (NIV): "From noon to three in the afternoon, darkness came over the land." Although this was the darkest time in human history, the glorious grace of God was exemplified by Jesus Christ's death on the cross because there could be no forgiveness of sin without the shedding of blood (Hebrews 9:22).

God transferred the sin of humanity to the sinless life of Christ and judged sin for all time on the cross. Because of Christ's death, burial and resurrection, we have been redeemed, or rescued, from God's wrath and enslavement to sin and its deadly consequences; and, we have received forgiveness of our sins, based on the riches of God's grace (Ephesians 1:7).

Because we have been forgiven, Jesus Christ now calls on us to forgive others who have sinned against us. Jesus included this command in the model prayer that He taught His disciples to pray to the Father, "…And forgive us our debts, as we forgive our debtors" (Matthew 6:12, KJV). Debts refer to our sins, trespasses, or wrongdoings. If we are not forgiven of our sins, a Holy God must punish us for our sins. However, First John 1:9 says that if we confess our sins, God is "faithful and just to forgive us our sins and to cleanse us from all unrighteousness." And, it is all because of Jesus Christ! According to Bible commentator, Matthew Henry:

> Our hearts' desire and prayer to our heavenly Father every day should be, that He would forgive us our debts; that the obligation to punishment may be cancelled and vacated... (We can rely on) the satisfaction made to the justice of God for the sin of man—by the dying of the Lord Jesus, our Surety.[1]

We Need God's Help to Forgive Others

By the time we get to the seventh prayer watch, which is in the middle of the day, we probably would have had plenty of opportunities to become offended. If so, this also means that we would have had plenty of opportunities to practice forgiveness. Jesus said that if we do not forgive others when they do wrong to us, neither will God forgive us when we ask His forgiveness for doing wrong to others (Matthew 6:14-15).

Forgiveness is not a natural human trait. In fact, it runs counter to our human nature. Rather than forgive those who hurt us, we would prefer being angry at the person who offended us, complaining about what happened to us, and seeking revenge! Yet, the Bible admonishes us in Ephesians 4:26, "Be angry and sin not. Do not let the sun go down while you are still angry." Notice that the verse recognizes that we will be angry at times. However, harboring anger may cause us to do something we should not do against the person who hurt us. This is why we have to learn how to release our anger.

But, how can we forgive someone when the pain we feel is sometimes too hard to bear? Imagine how the Jews felt when in the year 2000, Johannes Rau, the president of Germany at that time, stood before the Knesset (Israel's legislative body) to ask Israel to forgive Germany for the Holocaust during World War II. About six million European Jews died in Adolf Hitler's Nazi Germany from 1941 to 1945. In an emotionally charged speech, Rau, who spoke in German, said in part before the people of Israel:

> I pay humble tribute to those who were murdered, who have no graves at which I could ask their forgiveness. I ask forgiveness for what Germans have done—for myself and my generation, for the sake of our children and children's children, whose future I would like to see at the side of the children of Israel.
>
> We Germans, too, will be accompanied, for all time to come, by the images of the murders for which Germans bear responsibility. Between Germans and Israelis, this memory forges an inseparable link. The perpetrators take their personal guilt with them to their graves. But, the consequences of a guilt

that shook the very foundations of human morality must be borne by the generations to come.[2]

According to media reports, some Knesset legislators applauded politely while others boycotted the speech.[3]

The truth is, we cannot truly forgive others without God's supernatural help. Jesus Christ demonstrated forgiveness—even when He was in agony on the cross—by asking His Father to forgive those who crucified Him (Luke 23:34). Jesus wanted to show us how to call upon God to help us to forgive others "from the heart." What does "from the heart" mean? It means that we allow God to perform "supernatural surgery" on us and go deep within our heart to take away the sting from our hurt and heal our pain. This in no way means that we forget what has happened to us, but we do not carry the burden of hatred against those who have hurt us.

Jesus Christ did not hate those who abused Him, even though He had been betrayed by Judas, His own disciple, mocked by the Roman soldiers, and ridiculed by the Jewish leaders. As Jesus was dying on the cross between two thieves, and as the soldiers "cast lots" or gambled to see who would win His clothes, Jesus managed to say in His weakened physical state, "Father, forgive them, for they do not know what they do" (Luke 23:34).

If we do not follow Christ's example and be willing to truly forgive from the heart, we will eventually become trapped in the moment when the offense happened. Every time we relive the moment of someone hurting us, the pain and anger swells up again. We then, unknowingly, allow that person to have control over us and we cannot move forward with our lives. This is why forgiveness is not really about another person, it is about us. It is about starting the healing process and asking for God's help so that we can once again have peace.

Some people are afraid that if they forgive, they are allowing the person to "get away" with hurting them. However, forgiving someone does not mean that you condone what that person has done to hurt you. It means that you are surrendering your hurt to God and letting Him have the final say in the matter.

While we like to focus on what others have done to us, we seldom focus on what we may have done—intentionally or unintentionally—to others. Forgiving others and asking God and others to forgive us, breaks our pride and keeps us humble, according to Martin Luther, the German reformer:

> And let no one think that as long as we live here, he can reach a position that he will not need forgiveness. In short, if God does not forgive without ceasing, we are lost.[4]

As we submit ourselves to God, He will help us to release past offenses and let go of the pain. We will then be transformed by the power of forgiveness.

How to Effectively Pray for Forgiveness

If we want to maintain a solid relationship with God, we must not hold grudges against others who have hurt us. Moreover, if we have hurt someone else—intentionally or unintentionally—we must make it right with that person. Jesus said in Matthew 6:14-15, "For if you forgive men their trespasses, your heavenly Father will also forgive you. But if you do not forgive men their trespasses, neither will your Father forgive your trespasses."

To effectively pray a personal prayer of forgiveness during this prayer watch, you may consider following these steps:

1. Acknowledge, to God, how you feel towards the person who hurt or angered you. Do not pretend that the person's actions did not affect you.

2. Ask God to help you to forgive that person from your heart. This is not just a mental exercise in forgiveness. Forgiveness has to be from your very soul.

3. Ask the Holy Spirit to shine His Divine spotlight on your heart and show you if you did anything against the person who hurt you or if you did anything against someone else for which you stand in need of forgiveness.

4. Ask God for forgiveness for what you did and if the Holy Spirit directs you, ask the person to forgive you for what you have done.

5. Thank God that You are forgiven through the Blood of Jesus Christ, His Son.

6. Do not hold on to grudges. Release the person who did you harm and let them go, along with your pain and anger. Forgiveness is your path to peace of mind.

Sample Prayer for Forgiveness

Father, in Jesus Name, I bring my hurt, anger, and pain before you because of what (<u>name of person</u>) did to me (or because of an incident that happened to you). Father, help me to forgive (<u>name of person</u>) just as Jesus forgave those who turned against Him while dying on the cross.

Father, please forgive me for hurting others (<u>be specific about what you did</u>). Thank You for forgiving me through Jesus Christ. And, thank You Jesus, because if it were not for You, I could not be forgiven in the eyes of my Heavenly Father. In Jesus' Name, I pray this prayer of forgiveness, Amen.

Prayer for Salvation

Related Scriptures

John 3: 16-17; Acts 2:21

Scriptures to Use in Prayer

Romans 10:9-10,13

Strategic Times to Pray

Sixth Prayer Watch
9:00 a.m. – 12:00 noon

Seventh Prayer Watch
12:00 noon – 3:00 p.m.

Chapter Ten

During the sixth and seventh prayer watches, Jesus hung on the cross to purchase our salvation. Because of Jesus' sacrifice, we can now have a restored relationship with God, the Father, and live eternally with Him. Therefore, these are the watches in which we can pray for the salvation of our loved ones and friends. In the Bible, the word, "salvation" is used in the general sense to mean, "to be delivered," "to get help," or "to get victory." The word is found in many places in the Old Testament, particularly in scriptures where the writer is asking God for deliverance from his enemies.

In the Hebrew language, the word "yasha" is the root word for salvation, and the name, "Yeshuah" (yesh-shoo-aw) is derived from the word yasha. The name, Yeshuah is associated with God being the Deliverer, the One bringing salvation, as used in Psalm 68:19, "Blessed be the Lord, who daily loads us with benefits, the God of our salvation (Yeshuah)!" Interestingly, Yeshuah is the Hebrew name for "Joshua." And, the Greek form of the name, "Joshua" is "Jesus"—the true Salvation of the world (John 3:16-17).

There are several instances where the scriptures play on the Hebrew name, Yeshuah to associate salvation with

Jesus Christ. For instance, an Angel of the Lord told Joseph in Matthew 1:21, that his wife Mary would have a son and "you shall call His name, JESUS (Savior), for He will save His people from their sins." This is exactly what Jesus did on the cross of Calvary.

God accepted the Blood of Christ as the satisfying sacrifice for sin, which was first committed in the Garden of Eden by Adam and Eve (Genesis 3). As a result, a sacrifice had to be made to reconcile mankind back to God. Jesus Christ, the Second Adam, the sinless and perfect God-Man, willingly gave His life as the substitutional sacrifice for sin. Therefore, those who repent of their sins and accept Christ's substitutional sacrifice are reconciled to God and no longer have to pay the eternal punishment for sin, which is eternal separation from God, the Father:

> So we praise God for the glorious grace he has poured out on us who belong to his dear Son. He is so rich in kindness and grace that he purchased our freedom with the blood of his Son and forgave our sins. He has showered his kindness on us, along with all wisdom and understanding (Ephesians 1:6-8, NLT).

Eternal life is God's gift of grace to us, there is nothing that we can do to earn it. Ephesians 2:8-9 says, "For by grace have you been saved through faith, and that not of yourselves; it is the gift of God, not of works, lest, anyone should boast." American revivalist preacher, Jonathan Edwards says, "You contribute nothing to your salvation except the sin that made it necessary."

Charles H. Spurgeon also emphasized that there is nothing that we did to merit God's favor, it was all because of Jesus Christ:

> Let it never be forgotten that Jesus gives all that is needful for our salvation. It is highly important that all seekers after mercy should remember this. Faith is as much the gift of God as is the Savior upon whom that faith relies. Repentance of sin is as truly the work of grace as the making of an atonement by which sin is blotted out. Salvation, from first to last, is of grace alone.[1]

How to Effectively Pray for Salvation

When Christ died on the cross at 3:00 p.m., our sin debt to God was paid. As a result, God offers us His free gift of grace, but we must take the initiative to receive it. So, when we pray, we should ask God to do the following:

1. Bring those for whom we are praying to Christ. Jesus said in John 6:44 that no one can come to Him unless God, the Father, draws them, or pulls them to Christ with His love.

2. Give them spiritual insight so that they might grow in their knowledge of God (Ephesians 1:17).

3. Help them to understand the eternal inheritance God has for them through Jesus Christ and the incredible greatness of God's power for those who believe Him (Ephesians 1:18-20).

Sample Prayer for Salvation

The following is a sample prayer for salvation if you are leading someone to Christ:

Heavenly Father, I come to You in the Name of Jesus. I confess that I am a sinner and I am sorry for all the sinful things I have done in my life. I ask that You forgive me and wash away all of my sins, by the Blood of Your Son, Jesus Christ.

Father, Your Word says that if I confess with my mouth the Lord Jesus and believe in my heart that You have raised Him from the dead, I will be saved (Romans 10:9). Therefore, I confess Jesus Christ as the Lord of my life. I believe that He shed His precious blood on the cross at Calvary and died for my sins; and with my heart, I believe that You raised Him from the dead.

Now, Jesus, I ask You to come into my heart, fill me with Your Holy Spirit, and transform my life as I surrender to Your Divine Calling. In Jesus' name, Amen.

Prayer for Repentance

Related Scriptures

Ezekiel 18:21-23; Luke 13:3;
Acts 3:19, 17:30; 2 Peter 3:9

Scriptures to Use in Prayer

2 Chronicles 7:14; Psalm 38:18;
Proverbs 28:13; 1 John 1:9

Strategic Times to Pray

Sixth Prayer Watch
9:00 a.m. – 12:00 noon

Seventh Prayer Watch
12:00 noon – 3:00 p.m.

Chapter Eleven

About 9:00 a.m., the beginning of the sixth prayer watch, Jesus Christ was nailed to the cross, according to Mark 15:25. He remained on the cross until around 3:00 p.m., the end of the seventh prayer watch. Jesus faced an agonizing death so that the human race could be reconciled to God and live eternally with Him. To have this new life in Christ, we must first acknowledge that we have sinned against God and His laws, and repent of our sins. Once we accept Christ as the Lord and Savior of our lives, God releases us from the penalty of sin, which is eternal separation from Him. As we pray during this watch, we can ask the Holy Spirit if we need to repent of our actions so that we can make it right with God or with others that we may have offended.

Jesus hung on the cross between two thieves. At first, both thieves spoke abusively to Him, according to Matthew 27:44. However, Luke 23:39-43 says that one of the thieves had a change of heart and repented. He rebuked the other thief and told him that both of them were guilty of their crimes, but Jesus was innocent. He then said to Jesus, "Remember me when You come into Your kingdom" (vs. 42). Jesus replied, "Assuredly, I say to you, today you will be with Me in Paradise." The thief's willingness to repent while he was physically dying, resulted in his obtaining eternal life.

What is Repentance?

The word, "repent," is found in many places in the Bible. To repent means to have a change of mind or heart about a matter which results in a change of action. The picture is that of a person who is driving down the wrong road that leads to a dead end. After realizing he is going the wrong way, the driver decides to turn around to get back on the right road.

Repentance involves realizing how our actions have insulted God and other people. Repentance means not only grieving for the sins we committed, but abandoning the behaviors that caused us to sin in the first place. This is what the apostle Paul calls "godly sorrow" (2 Corinthians 7:10-11).

The key to true repentance is not about feeling sorry for what we have done, but what we do as a result of that sorrow. It is possible to be sorry for a wrongdoing but show no true signs of repentance. For instance, Jesus' disciple, Judas, acknowledged that he betrayed Jesus. When Judas saw that Jesus was condemned to die, Matthew 27:4 (KJV) says that Judas "repented." The Greek word for repented in this verse is "metamelomai," which means "being remorseful" or "having an element of repentance," but not necessarily being truly repentant. [1] While Judas may have felt remorseful, apparently he was not truly repentant and committed suicide. On the other hand, Peter, another one of Jesus' disciples, denied knowing Jesus three times prior to His crucifixion, and Peter "wept bitterly" over what he had done (Matthew 26:75, Mark 14:72, Luke 22:62). However, as a result of Peter's true repentance, Jesus forgave Peter for his denial (John 21:15-18) and Peter went on to become the leader of Jesus' apostles.

There is a worldly sorry, which Judas had, and a godly sorrow, which Peter experienced. According to author Alexander MacLaren, the question is: "Which sorrow makes us change our attitude?":

> The one kind of sorrow, which measures my sin by the side of the brightness and purity of God, vindicates itself as true, because it makes me hate my evil and turn away from it. The other, which is of the world, passes over me like the empty wind through an archway, it whistles for a moment and is gone, and there is nothing left to show that it was ever there…Godly sorrow works a change of attitude, purpose, and mind; the sorrow of the world leaves a man standing where he was. Ask yourselves the question: Which of the two are you familiar with? [2]

Repentance Goes Beyond Individuals

While repentance is associated with personal salvation, the Bible also shows that repentance can extend beyond one person to the nations. The Old Testament prophets would call entire nations to repentance. In the first chapter of the book of Jonah, God told the prophet to preach against the city of Ninevah and announce His judgment against the people because their wicked deeds had come to His attention (Jonah 1:2).

When Jonah told the people that Ninevah would be destroyed in 40 days, the King of Ninevah led the people in a citywide fast (which even included the animals) and instructed them to "turn" (have a change of mind) or repent of their sins and "give up their evil ways and their violence" (Jonah 3:8, NIV). As a result, God, in His great mercy, spared the city because of the people's repentance.

God promises salvation and eternal life to individuals who personally repent and accept Jesus Christ. God also promises to bless nations that acknowledge Him. 2 Peter 3:9 says, God is merciful and is not "willing that any should perish but that all should come to repentance."

How to Effectively Pray a Prayer of Repentance

As you pray during the sixth and seventh prayer watches, ask the Holy Spirit to shine His Divine light on your heart to reveal whether you need to repent about a certain matter. If you do, the following is an example of the steps to take toward repentance:

1. Confess that you have committed sin. If you are interceding on behalf of an individual or nation, you can confess the sin of the individual or nation. The Bible gives plenty of examples of prophets and civil and religious leaders repenting on behalf of themselves and others (See 2 Samuel 12:13; 1 Chronicles 21; Jeremiah 3:6; Daniel 9:3-19).

2. Be specific about the type of sin committed.

3. Renounce the sin and ask God for His mercy and forgiveness. If you are interceding for an individual or a nation, ask God to help that person or nation to renounce or reject their sin.

4. Ask the Holy Spirit to show you how you can change your attitude and abandon the behavior that caused you to repent.

Sample Prayer of Repentance

Father, in the Name of Jesus, Your Word says in 1 John 1:9 that if I confess my sin, You are faithful and just to forgive me of my sin and cleanse me from all my unrighteous acts.

Now, Father, I repent of (<u>confess the specific reason for repentance</u>). I acknowledge my sin and ask for Your forgiveness.

Holy Spirit, I ask You to help me change my mind and abandon the behavior that has placed me in this circumstance.

Lord, I want to make it right with You and those whom I have offended (<u>Name the person or people and what you did to them</u>).

I accept Your cleansing power in my life and thank You for Your restoration, in Jesus' Name, Amen.

Prayer for Boldness

Related Scriptures

1 Samuel 17:45; Nehemiah 6:11;
Daniel 6:10; Acts 9:27-29, 18:26, 19:8;
Ephesians 3:12; Philippians 1:14

Scriptures to Use in Prayer

Acts 4:29-30, Ephesians 6:19

Strategic Time to Pray

Eighth Prayer Watch
3:00 p.m. – 6:00 p.m.

Chapter Twelve

Jesus Christ's death on the cross during the eighth prayer watch established a New Covenant between God and His highest creation, mankind (Matthew 27:45-51). Under this New Covenant, Believers in Jesus Christ have spiritual power and authority through the Holy Spirit Who comforts and advocates for His people (John 16:13). Jesus told His disciples that the Holy Spirit would give them power—authority, ability, and courage—to carry the gospel throughout the world (Acts 1:8).

Jesus Christ's Great Commission applies to us, also, His present-day disciples. We also must depend on the Holy Spirit to carry out our God-given assignments. This means that we need to pray for boldness.

There will be times when opposition will come against us because we speak the Name of Jesus as we exercise our spiritual authority. Because of this, during this watch, we will need to pray for boldness. The book of Acts shows us examples of how the power of God prevails despite opposition. We see in Acts 3:1 where Peter and John were on their way to the Temple in Jerusalem at 3:00 p.m. (which was the hour of prayer and the beginning of the eighth prayer watch), when they saw a lame man lying at one of the Temple gates called, the "Beautiful Gate." Peter and John were among the 120 believers who received the infilling of the Holy Spirit in the Upper Room on the day of Pentecost. Peter and John exercised their new spiritual authority and commanded the lame man to "rise up and walk," in the Name of Jesus (Acts 3:6). The people marveled over the miraculous healing.

However, the priests, the captain of the temple, and the Sadducees were upset with Peter for telling the crowd that the lame man was healed through his faith in the Name of Jesus (Acts 3:16). As a result, the Jewish religious and civil leaders arrested Peter and John and later commanded them "not to speak at all nor teach in the name of Jesus" (Acts 4:18). But, the Holy Spirit gave the two apostles boldness to tell the group that they would continue to speak about Jesus Christ.

After their release, Peter and John went back to their fellow believers to report to them what happened. Encouraged by the testimony of Peter and John, the group prayed and asked God for "all boldness" to speak His Word (Acts 4:29).

The apostle Paul also prayed for boldness to proclaim the gospel. You would think that Paul already possessed courage based on all of the hardships he endured (1 Corinthians 4:9-13). Nonetheless, we see in Ephesians 6:19-20 (NLT) that Paul, while in jail, asked the Christians in Ephesus to pray that God would give him boldness to continue carrying out his divine assignment:

> And pray for me, too. Ask God to give me the right words so I can boldly explain God's

mysterious plan that the Good News is for Jews and Gentiles alike. I am in chains now, still preaching this message as God's ambassador. So pray that I will keep on speaking boldly for him, as I should.

Paul had a continual need to pray for boldness because of his divine calling as an apostle. Paul was asking for prayer so that he might have courage to speak the truth of God clearly, freely and in love (Ephesians 4:15).

There has always been opposition to the gospel of Jesus Christ, from the time of the apostles to our present day. As a matter of fact, the apostle Paul said, "All who desire to live godly in Christ Jesus will suffer persecution" (2 Timothy 3:12). Nonetheless, God will give supernatural boldness to those who choose to live for Him and carry out their God-given assignments even at the cost of their lives.

How to Effectively Pray for Boldness

To pray effectively during the eighth prayer watch so that we will be able to boldly carry out God's work and exercise our spiritual authority in Jesus Christ, we can use the same prayer that was prayed by the believers in Acts 4:23-30 as a pattern:

1. **Pray in unity.** If we are praying with a group, there should be no division among its members. According to Acts 4:24, after hearing about Peter and John's imprisonment and release, the group "raised their voice to God with one accord."

2. **Begin with praise and worship.** Whenever we pray, we should begin by praising and worshiping God who gives us the authority through Jesus Christ to carry out our Kingdom assignments. Peter's group began their prayer by worshiping God and His greatness, "Lord, You are God, who made heaven and earth and the sea, and all that is in them…" (Acts 4:24).

3. **Declare scripture.** We should read God's Word to find Bible scriptures that relate to boldness and use our Divine authority to carry out God's work. In Acts 4:25-26, we see where Peter's group quoted Psalm 2:1-2 that related to the issue that they were facing at that moment.

4. **Be specific in your request.** We should be specific in our prayer requests. Although our requests may be personal, we should make sure that what we want ultimately glorifies God and Jesus Christ. As they continued in prayer, Peter and the other believers asked God for boldness, "Now, Lord, look on their threats, and grant to Your servants that with all boldness they may speak Your word,

by stretching out Your hand to heal, and that signs and wonders may be done through the name of Your holy Servant Jesus" (Acts 4: 27-30).

After we pray, with the authority Jesus Christ has given us, we still must wait for God to answer our prayer. While we may not get the answer that we were expecting—or the miraculous way in which God answered Peter's group—we must continue to have confidence that He has heard us and trust God to respond in a way that gives Him the glory and us the boldness that we need:

> And when they had prayed, the place where they were assembled together was shaken; and they were all filled with the Holy Spirit, and they spoke the word of God with boldness (Acts 4:31).

Sample Prayer for Boldness

Father, in the Name of Jesus, I pray for boldness to speak Your Word and exercise the spiritual authority that I have through Jesus Christ.

Father, I ask You to give me the courage to speak Your truth with force and directness, and in love. I do not depend on my own natural abilities, but I depend upon Your Holy Spirit to show me what to say and when to say it.

As an ambassador for Jesus Christ, I pray the same prayer as the apostles that You would grant me boldness to speak Your Word, and that You will stretch out Your hand with healing power so that miracles can take place through the name of Your Holy Son, Jesus Christ, Amen.

About the Author

United in Christ Ministries of Canton, Michigan, is a marketplace ministry designed to reflect God's love by helping men and women become grounded in the life principles and spiritual truths of the Bible. Our goal is to help fulfil the Great Commission of Christ: "Go ye therefore and teach all nations" (Matthew 28:19).

Visit our website: https://unitedinchristcanton.org

Follow us on Twitter: www.twitter.com/uicm2009

Endnotes

Introduction

1. United in Christ Ministries of Canton, *Watch and Pray: Understanding the Eight Prayer Watches* (*United in Christ Ministries of Canton*, 2013).

2. Albert Barnes, *Notes on the New Testament*, http://www.ccel.org/ccel/barnes/ntnotes.i.html (accessed December 1, 2017).

3. ibid.

4. Albert Barnes, *Notes on the New Testament*, http://www.ccel.org/ccel/barnes/ntnotes.xxii.xi.vi.html (accessed December 13, 2017).

5. George Müller, *Answers to Prayer*, https://www.georgemuller.org/uploads/4/8/6/5/48652749/_answers_to_prayer_book.pdf(accessed December 13, 2017).

6. ibid.

Chapter One: Intercessory Prayer

1. Tony M. Anderson, *Prayer Availeth Much*, http://www.ccel.org/ccel/anderson/prayer.xi.html (accessed December 1, 2017).

2. J.E. Hutton, *A History of the Moravian Church*, http://www.ccel.org/ccel/hutton/moravian.v.iii.html (accessed December 1, 2017).

3. Tony M. Anderson, *Prayer Availeth Much*, http://www.ccel.org/ccel/anderson/prayer.xi.html (accessed December 1, 2017).

Chapter Two: Prayer for Healing

1. Alfred Edersheim, *Life and Times of Jesus the Messiah*, http://www.ccel.org/ccel/edersheim/lifetimes.viii.xxvi.html (accessed December 2, 2017).

2. C.H. Spurgeon, *Songs in the Night*, http://www.biblebb.com/files/spurgeon/2558.htm (accessed December 2, 2017).

3. Daystar.com, "Dodie Osteen—Trust, Fear and the Everlasting Love of Jesus," https//www.daystar.com/news-updates/general-updates/dodie-osteen-trust-fear-and-the-everlasting-love-of-jesus/ (accessed December 2, 2017

4. ibid.

5. "Birth of a Song: A True Story" by Thomas A. Dorsey, http://www.inspire21.com/stories/faithstories/Precious Lord (accessed December 14, 2017).

6. ibid.

Chapter Three: Prayer of Thanksgiving

1. Edward M. Bounds, *Essentials of Prayer*, http://www.ccel.org/ccel/bounds/essentials.v.html?highlight=thanksgiving,praise,and,worship#highlight (accessed December 2, 2017).

2. Ibid.

Chapter Four: Prayer of Petition

1. James Orr, M.A., D.D. General Editor, *International Standard Bible Encyclopedia*, 1915, https://www.ml biblestudytools.com/encyclopedias/isbe/importunity.ht (accessed December 3, 2017).

2. Tony M. Anderson, *Prayer Availeth Much*, https://www.ccel.org/ccel/anderson/prayer.xi.html (accessed December 3, 2017)

3. Wikipedia contributors, "Dunkirk evacuation" *Wikipedia, The Free Encyclopedia,* https://en.wikipedia.org/wiki/Dunkirk_evacuation (accessed December 21, 2017).

Chapter Six: Prayer for Protection

1. Wikipedia contributors, "Wall Street bombing," Wikipedia, The Free Encyclopedia, https://en.wikipedia.org/wiki/Wall_Street_bombing (accessed March 10, 2018).

2. Kathy S. Wilson, *The Faithfulness of Our God* (Kathy S. Wilson, 2016).

Chapter Seven: Spiritual Warfare Prayer

1. James E. Orr, *How to Live a Holy Life,* https://lcoggt.org/Orr/ho46.htm (accessed March 8, 2018).

2. Charles H. Spurgeon, *Christ's Prayer for Peter,* Spurgeon's Sermons Volume 45:1899, http://www.ccel.org/ccel/spurgeon/sermons45.xviii.html?highlight=sift,you,like,wheat#highlight (accessed December 1, 2017).

3. J.C. Ryle, *Holiness: Its Nature, Hindrances, Difficulties, and*

Roots, http://www.ccel. Org/ccel/ryle/holiness.iii.iv. html?highlight=spiritual,warfare#highlight (accessed December 1, 2017).

Chapter Eight: Prayer for Direction

1. Charles H. Spurgeon, *Ordered Steps,* Spurgeon's Sermons Volume 42:1896, http://www.ccel.org/ccel/spurgeon/sermons42.xlii.html?highlight=order,my, steps#highlight (accessed December 1, 2017).

2. Edward M. Bounds, *Power Through Prayer*, http://www.ccel.org/ccel/bounds/power.IX.html? (accessed December 1, 2017).

3. Edward M. Bounds, *Essentials of Prayer*, http://www.ccel.org/ccel/bounds/essentials.ix.html?highlight=consecration#highlight (accessed December 1, 2017).

4. Newman Hall, *The Bible Illustrator-Divine Guidance in the Midst of Dangers,"* https:// www.studylight.org/commentary/matthew/6-13.html (accessed December 1, 2017).

Chapter Nine: Prayer for Forgiveness

1. Matthew Henry, *Commentary on the Whole Bible*

Volume V (Matthew to John), http://www.ccel.org/ccel/henry/mhc5.Matt.vii.html (accessed December 2, 2017).

2. "Speech in the Knesset by the President of Germany, Johannes Rau", https://knesset.gov.il/description/eng/doc/speech_rau_2000_eng.pdf (accessed December 2, 2017).

3. "German President Asks Forgiveness For Holocaust," Sun Sentinel, February 17, 2000, http//articles.sun-sentinel.com/2000-02-17/news/-0002161140_1_german-president-rau-s-speech-far-right-leader (accessed December 2, 2017).

4. Martin Luther, *The Large Catechism*, http://www.ccel.org/ccel/luther/largecatechism.vi_1.html?highlight=god,forgiveness#highlight (accessed December 2, 2017).

Chapter Ten: Prayer for Salvation

1. Charles H. Spurgeon, *All of Grace-An Earnest Word with Those Who Are Seeking Salvation by the Lord Jesus Christ*, http://www.ccel.org /ccel/spurgeon/grace.xvi.html (accessed December 2, 2017).

Chapter Eleven: Prayer of Repentance

1. Louis Berkhof, *Systematic Theology*, http://www.ccel.org/ccel/berkhof/systematictheology.vi.vii.html?highlight=metamelomai# highlight (accessed December 2, 2017).

2. Alexander MacLaren, *Expositions of Holy Scripture: Second Corinthians, Galatians, and Philippians Chapters 1 to End*, http://www.ccel. org/ccel/maclaren/iicor_tim.ii.i.ii.html?highlight=the,other,which,is,of, world,passes,over,me,like,empty,wind,through,an, archway#highlight (accessed December 2, 2017).

The Art of Spiritual Warfare: A Manual

Elizabeth Cobbs, a journalist and associate with United in Christ Ministries of Canton, has written a clear and concise book to help Believers in Christ understand spiritual warfare and how to effectively use spiritual weapons in their daily lives. By offering strategies and tactics on how to handle satanic attacks head-on, you will learn how to wage a good warfare through Jesus Christ.

United in Christ
Ministries of Canton

Watch and Pray: Understanding the Eight Prayer Watches

This book will encourage you to pray strategically to defeat the Enemy and access all that God has for you in Christ Jesus. Also, this book answers the following questions:

- Why is prayer important?
- What is a prayer watch?
- What is a watchman?
- What are the time intervals for each prayer watch?
- What spiritual activities are involved during the eight prayer watches?

God's Divine Calendar
Understanding the Biblical Months

This book reveals the spiritual significance of each biblical month and how each month ultimately points to our Messiah, Jesus Christ.

You will develop a deeper appreciation for the Bible as you perceive it in a different way each month. You will also see God's hand consistently at work through the biblical calendar which He has established to bless His people.

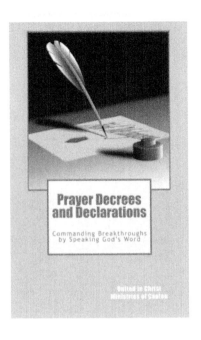

Prayer Decrees and Declarations

This book shares the importance of activating decrees and declarations in your prayer life. You will discover how proclaiming the Word of God releases your faith and takes you into higher spiritual dimensions.

Speaking the declarations and decrees in this book will motivate you to establish your own proclamations from God's Word. Most importantly, this book will enhance your spiritual growth and draw you into deeper relationship with God.

Made in the USA
Middletown, DE
09 June 2022